Destroying the Jezebel Spirit

How to Overcome the Spirit Before It Destroys You!

Bill Vincent

© 2016 by Bill Vincent.

All rights reserved. No part of this book may be reproduced, stored in a retrieval system or transmitted in any form or by any means without the prior written permission of the publishers, except by a reviewer who may quote brief passages in a review to be printed in a newspaper, magazine or journal.

Second Printing

Revival Waves of Glory Books & Publishing has allowed this work to remain exactly as the author intended, verbatim, without editorial input.

All Scripture quotations are from the Authorized King James Version of the Bible unless otherwise noted.

Softcover 978-1-68411-052-0

Hardcover 978-1-68411-053-7

PUBLISHED BY REVIVAL WAVES OF GLORY BOOKS & PUBLISHING
www.revivalwavesofgloryministries.com
Litchfield, IL

Printed in the United States of America

Table of Contents

Introduction 7
Chapter One **War Revealed** 9
Chapter Two **Describing Jezebel In History** 13
Chapter Three **Jezebel In Our Society** 17
Chapter Four **Network of Demons** 41
Chapter Five **Self-Centeredness** 45
Chapter Six **Jezebel's Identity** 49
Chapter Seven **Knowing Jezebel** 53
Chapter Eight **God's Covenant** 71
Chapter Nine **Characteristics of Jezebel** 79
Chapter Ten **Strongholds of Jezebel** 97
Chapter Eleven **Control of Jezebel** 101
Chapter Twelve **Dealing With Jezebel** 115
Chapter Thirteen **Jezebel and Divorce** 121
Chapter Fourteen **The Jezebel Culture** 129
Chapter Fifteen **Wounds and Jezebel** 139
Chapter Sixteen **The Power of the Jehu Mantle** ... 149
Chapter Seventeen **False Prophecy and Jezebel** ... 159
Chapter Eighteen **The Seduction of Jezebel** 171
Chapter Nineteen **Evil Strategies of Jezebel** 179
Chapter Twenty **Destroying the Spirit of Jezebel** ... 201
Chapter Twenty One **Dealing With Jezebel?** 207

Prayer	217
About the Author	221
Warfare Books	223
Recommended Books	225

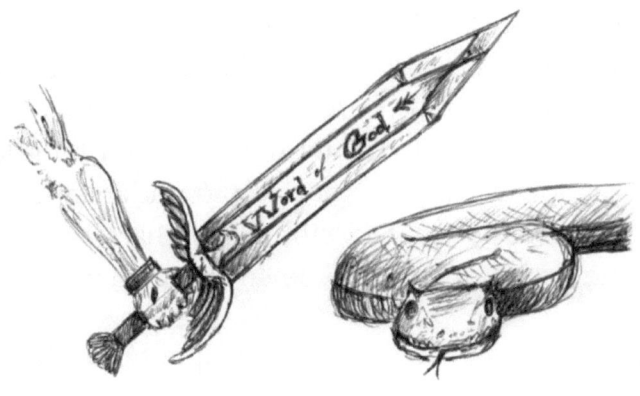

Introduction

In my over 20 years of ministry, there has been countless spirits and demons that I have personally been allowed by God's grace to overcome in many people's lives. There have been various kinds but none as dangerous as the spirit of Jezebel.

This book is as no other I have written because of the history of dealing with this spirit so many times over the years. I don't think we need to take this lightly. I will repeat myself, but it is to bring clarity. Some need to read every word and study the scriptures supplied and some have received much revelation on this spirit and don't need the foundational truths. I want to tell you, don't just skim the surface because there is much that the Holy Spirit is releasing through this book. In the years, I have learned a great deal more about this principality, this strongman, and how it operates. After writing "Defeating the Demonic Realm" I never thought I would be releasing a book of this power again. I want you to understand failure to address the weaknesses and sinful responses have wreaked havoc in the lives of men and women everywhere.

In explaining the Jezebel principality, its history and how it operates. Jezebel spirit of control functions through leaders in positions of spiritual authority. I place strong emphasis on how a Jezebel spirit is genderless, this principality operates in both males and females—often differently, but without question doing its evil work in both genders.

All Christians must face up to the fact that their real battle is with their flesh. The power of the flesh, which is capable of opposing the Holy Spirit in all He wants to do, far exceeds the "power" of the enemy. Jesus has already dealt a death blow to Satan! Now He desires to rule from the throne He has established at the center of our lives. All flesh must submit to His Kingship.

God's goal for each of us is maturity. He works with us to bring us to the fullness of His likeness.

Satan's wiles; they are not new. They include twisting the truth of Scripture, fear mongering, manipulation of wounded egos and many more strategies that fill Jezebel's bag of tricks. This principality uses all these to gain control through "little Jezebels," whose mental repetition is I am always on my mind.

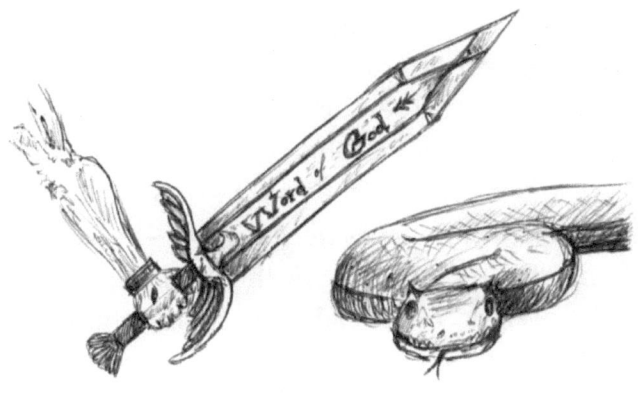

Chapter One

War Revealed

Whether everyone will admit it or not we are in a war. The battle line has been drawn and we must stand up and fight when necessary. In this scripture the apostle Paul, speaking about the spiritual conflict believers in Christ constantly are engaged in, says these words in Ephesians 6:12:

> Ephesians 6:12 For we wrestle not against flesh and blood, but against principalities, against powers, against the rulers of the darkness of this world, against spiritual wickedness in high places.

Make no mistake, though. We are at war. Princes and powers are real, and they love nothing better than for us to deny their influence and remain ignorant of their significance. When carnal Christians say that Paul is not speaking of the demonic realm when he teaches on it in Ephesians 6, and that these are not spiritual beings he refers to—personalities with a will of their own—I want to ask them which Christ they are following. Those who follow Jesus Christ, the Christ of the gospels, will engage their archenemies by wrestling with them in their walk in the Spirit. The Greek word arche, translated in the verse above as "rulers" or "principalities," refers to those entities that have the highest rank in hell's government under their leader, Satan.

Jezebel is more than the name of a wicked queen who lived at a time of great spiritual decline in the history of God's chosen people. Jezebel is also a spiritual threat to those leaders whose assignment has been to nullify this demonic principality's power in the earth. The prophet Elijah's intense battle with this principality, this archenemy, is legendary. Elijah confronted Jezebel—both the human queen and the spiritual entity—at the height of his spiritual development, destroying her organized "system" that ruled the minds and behaviors of the masses, lulling them into a drunken stupor, leaving them blinded to the truth and demands of the Only Wise God.

Jezebel's footprint appears many times in Scripture, and many times in history.

The Holy Spirit intends for you to be fully aware, fully equipped and fully furnished in this hour, because as it was in the days of Elijah, so it is today that a fresh move of God's

Spirit is stirring amongst the truly hungry. God is whispering in their hearts that Jezebel must come down. So I entreat you to give heed to the words of this book . . . it will take you a long way in the Spirit.

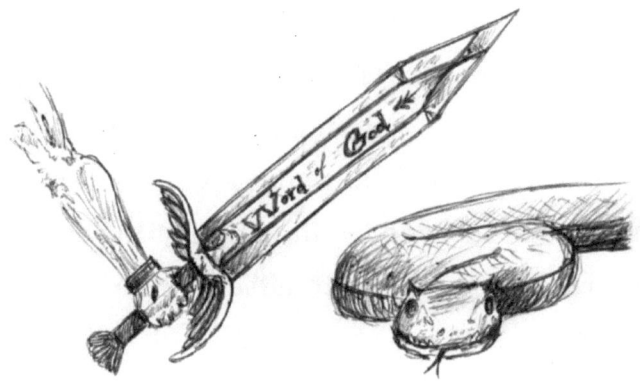

Chapter Two
Describing Jezebel In History

You wouldn't believe all the different opinions about the spirit of Jezebel. There is a variety of opinions about what constitutes a Jezebel spirit, everything from a sexually loose woman to someone—man or woman who teaches false doctrine. The Bible does not mention a Jezebel spirit, although it has plenty to say about Jezebel herself.

Jezebel is found in 1st and 2nd Kings. She was the daughter of Ethbaal, king of Tyre/Sidon and priest of the cult of Baal, a cruel, sensuous and revolting false god whose worship involved sexual filth and lewdness. Ahab, king of Israel, married Jezebel and led the nation into Baal worship (1 Kings 16:31). Their reign over Israel is one of the saddest chapters in the history of God's people.

There are two incidents in the life of Jezebel which characterize her and may define what is meant by the Jezebel spirit. One trait is her obsessive passion for domineering and controlling others, especially in the spiritual realm. When she became queen, she began a relentless campaign to rid Israel of all evidences of God's worship. She ordered the killing of all the prophets of God (1 Kings 18:4, 13) and replaced their altars with those of Baal. Her strongest enemy was Elijah who demanded a contest on Mount Carmel between the powers of Israel's Mighty One and the powers of Jezebel and the priests of Baal (1 Kings 18). Of course there was no contest, but despite hearing of the miraculous powers of God, Jezebel refused to repent and swore on her gods that she would pursue Elijah relentlessly and take his life. Her stubborn refusal to see and submit to the power of the living Elohim (Mighty One) would lead her to a hideous end (2 Kings 9:29-37).

The second incident involves a righteous man named Naboth who refused to sell to Ahab land adjoining the palace, rightly declaring that to sell his inheritance would be against God's command (1 Kings 21:3; Leviticus 25:23). While Ahab sulked and fumed on his bed, Jezebel taunted him and ridiculed him for his weakness, then proceeded to have the innocent Naboth framed and stoned to death. Naboth's sons were also stoned to death, so there would be no heirs and the land would revert to the possession of the king. Such a single-minded determination to have one's way, no matter who is destroyed in the process, is a characteristic of the Jezebel spirit.

So infamous was Jezebel's sexual immorality and idol worship that the Master Yeshua Himself refers to her in a warning to the church at Thyatira (Revelation 2:18-29). Most likely referring to a woman in the church who influenced it the same way Jezebel influenced Israel into idolatry and sexual immorality, the Lord declares to the Thyatirans that she is not to be tolerated. Whoever this woman was, like Jezebel she refused to repent of her immorality and her false teaching, and her fate was sealed. God cast her onto a sick bed, along with those who committed idolatry with her. The end for those who succumb to a Jezebel spirit is always death and destruction, both in the physical and the spiritual sense.

Perhaps the best way to define the Jezebel spirit is to say it characterizes anyone who acts in the same manner as Jezebel did, engaging in immorality, idolatry, false teaching and unrepentant sin. I want you to understand that it doesn't end there. Many spirits just like Jezebel have risen in this day. She was more than a person.

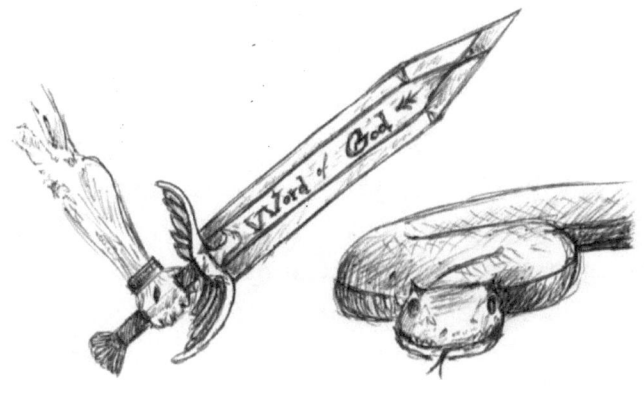

Chapter Three
Jezebel In Our Society

If your reading this book, you probably realize that the Spirit of Jezebel does exist. It can be difficult for some to take the Biblical picture of Jezebel and place that in our lives today. Jezebel was an actual person. Jezebel, the Biblical character, first appears in First Kings 16, when she marries Ahab, king of Israel. Jezebel was the daughter of Ethbaal, the king and high priest of the Baal worshipping Sidonians. Baal worship was closely associated with obsessive sensuality and often involved sex acts. Jezebel, as a daughter of this perverse kingdom, was raised in an atmosphere where sex was a path to power and influence.

Ahab, King of Israel, was completely subdued and dominated by Jezebel (a type of modern man). Jezebel then introduced the worship of Ashtoroth to Israel. This god/goddess, represented the Canaanite culture of the moon, was a power-hungry goddess of love and sensuality. Priestess-prostitutes filled her shrines and serviced her worshippers. The lure of these legal, readily available erotic encounters was more than the men of Israel would resist. By Jezebel's influence, most Israelites, the northern kingdom, left the worship of Yahweh for Baal and Ashtoroth. The prophet Elijah laments that only 7000 men in the entire nation were not swayed by her control.

The Jezebel spirit is born of witchcraft and rebellion. This demon is one of the most common spirits in operation today, both in the church and in the world, and it is a powerful enemy of the Body of Christ. She operates freely on sincere believers whose hearts are for the Lord individually, and has also attained positions of power as powers and principalities within the Church. This spirit establishes its stronghold primarily in women; however, many men have been victimized by it as well, where it functions as a "controlling" spirit.

The Spirit of Jezebel is basically a controlling spirit working through the lust of the flesh, and the lust of the eyes, and the pride of life. It has, in general, two aims:

- To gain identity, glory, recognition, power, and satisfy the need for the "praises of men." This is

a consequence of the desire for love and self-worth focused on SELF.
- Secondly the Jezebel spirit is a men hater and seeks to emasculate all men, and deny them of their authority and power over others. It raises a distrust and hatred of men in general. The "Jezebel spirit" is in a constant agitation, terribly aggressive, very determined, callous, controlling, selfish, power hungry, manipulative, unrepentant, deceitful spirit, an overwhelmingly evil spirit, and those are mostly only it's good points! Indeed this spirit can be definitely named "Satan's woman".

There are two main types of the Jezebel spirit:

- The high-profile type is generally gregarious (very friendly and sociable), outspoken and highly visible. She is often seen as the "woman who wears the pants in the family".
- The low-profile type is soft-spoken, giving the illusion of being considerate (1. Expressing an attitude of concern and consideration 2. Full of eagerness to do something 3. Paying very careful attention to details), motherly, protective, even appearing very submissive.

This profile type may be the most dangerous, as she is the most difficult to discern. She relies heavily on manipulation for her power, in extremely subtle performances.

Here are some basic characteristics to look at and we will look at more later. Within these two main types there are two manifestations: the seducer and the cool.

The seducer uses any type of seduction available to gain control and power, as a method of manipulation but specializes in spiritual seduction to operate on both males and females. Her seduction usually uses subtle flattery and her seduction is spiritual fornication. Men are particularly blind and easy victims to the subtleties of this seduction, as she flatters them with her attention. Women seduced by the Jezebel spirit are blinded to their own seduction, as they do not expect it, or are not aware of such manipulation.

A good example of the cool Jezebel spirit personality can frequently be seen as the efficient (and often plain) executive assistant at the side of a powerful businessman or church leader. This Jezebel spirit often lacks a gregarious personality, but may be very outspoken and aggressive.

Some of this spirit's features are as follows:

Deceiver

This spirit works in "private," people outside her circle hardly know her maneuvering and are an easy pray for manipulation. Those that are possessed by her tend to defend her from any form of criticism. Like many men today defend feminism.

Man-Hater

The Jezebel spirit hates men and majors in destroying them. She cannot have a true Godly relationship with men; because her desire is to strip them of all their perceived power and then destroy them, to emasculate them emotionally and spiritually.

Un-submitted

The Jezebel spirit reviles (despises and shows no respect for) authority over her. Building on "dislike of authority" (especially of men since they are frequently the authority figure) coupled with rebellion, she hates anyone placed in authority over her (particularly men), and seeks to destroy them and take their power. The Jezebel spirit sees herself as the "goddess on the pedestal."

Power-Hungry

The Jezebel spirit is extremely power-hungry, respecting only power stronger than her own. She disdains or considers herself superior to anyone she perceives as having no power, or power less than hers. She works through her conquest to attain power over others.

Intelligent

This spirit from hell is very intelligent and finds very challenging to control and manipulate intellectually able people. She is able to manipulate them so well that actually they worship her.

Hard Worker

The Jezebel spirit frequently sees themselves as being "super achievers," which sadly is admired both in the church and business world. She is also a master in hindering others to achieve anything, kind of: doing everything she can to prevent others from achieving their set goals and then criticizes them for not having achieved these aims.

Self Worship

Internally the Jezebel spirit worships herself even though externally she may portray a picture of humility and submission. She is very proud of herself and extremely vain, and in her pride can only talk about herself. They are usually very attractive and they use that to seduce their victims.

Jealous

She cannot suffer others getting attention over herself and she will do all she can to prevent others receiving attention and recognition. If one gets between the Jezebel spirit and the person she is trying to control, she'll attack most viciously, trying her best to destroy that relationship with that person. She will try and destroy his reputation, undermine his authority and generally stop at nothing to separate anyone from her intended "victim." Beware!

Manipulator

The Jezebel spirit uses other people as objects, where it suits her need, to gain control, influence and power. Once she has gained the control desired, she generally rejects and tosses the people aside. If they are in her family, she does this emotionally.

Queen Bee

The Jezebel spirit demands worship from others. She must have dominance and control in her home. Other family members exist just to please her. The Jezebel spirit requires "worship" from her family and followers ... to be their "goddess".

Domineering

The Jezebel spirit is extremely authoritarian ("bossy") by nature, though subtly with the low profile type. She is easily offended if her authority is questioned, and will often respond with extreme anger at even the slightest offence. She demands blind loyalty.

Unrealistic Expectations of Others

Her expectations of others are always unrealistic, because others cannot meet her demand for complete submission. If they do try, she despises them and casts them aside when she has what she wants out of them. Anyone attempting to relate to a person with this spirit is literally in a "no-win situation." Nothing pleases this spirit.

Perfectionist

Perfectionism is a common characteristic of the Jezebel spirit, generating self-hatred in the victim, and a despising of others around her who fail to meet her exaggerated standards. This is part of the "unrealistic expectations" she has toward herself and others, but it is also an excuse for disrespect toward others, especially those in authority since they don't "measure up" so she doesn't have to show respect, of course.

Seduction, Control, Manipulation

Control and manipulation are the strongest parts of the Jezebel nature. These are "spirits of witchcraft" and are extremely dangerous! Nearly everything the Jezebel spirit does utilizes one or both spirits to attain her goal. The Jezebel spirit is the ultimate manipulator. The adulterous woman says:

> Proverbs 30:20 Such *is* the way of an adulterous woman; she eateth, and wipeth her mouth, and saith, I have done no wickedness.

The first step in someone who has the Jezebel spirit is they work to control their victim by seduction. She will use flattery, smooth prophetic sayings, pleasant words and seducing tears. She views children in a marriage as tools and weapons to manipulate hubby and family.

She knows how to use deep emotional hurts and wounds to manipulate and control as she creates apparent deep ties with others. Jezebel loves to pull people unto herself and away from those who can truly speak into their lives. The Jezebel spirit flows best in a whirlwind of confusion and turmoil, where she works best.

Shark

The Jezebel spirit is like a shark; she is most vicious and dangerous. She circles the lives of others looking for teachable, seducible, controllable, "disciples" of her own. The Jezebel spirit likes to birth spiritual children of her own as she looks for disciples to eat from her own table. She will look for those that are in rebellion, who are weak, wounded, or those who are contending, bucking, and fighting any established spiritual authority.

Possessive

The Jezebel spirit is very possessive and domineering; she wants to control over others. The Jezebel spirit loves power, "Give me, give me, give me." You see, money is not really the issue with this spirit; it's power and authority that she's after. She likes to be in control of others life because she draws her strength from controlling others. She spiritually drains her victims. She uses faults or weaknesses she perceives in the person she is attempting to control to create feelings of shame or guilt, and therefore ultimately submission to her will. She also often uses fear and intimidation to manipulate others into submission to her.

Self-pity

She uses self-pity and her own weaknesses to manipulate another into submitting to her out of compassion or pity. Feeling sorry for those who has this Jezebel spirit, is not compassion, it's foolishness!

Even though often very gifted of God, the Jezebel spirit will frequently operate in the false discernment of the enemy by speaking words of knowledge gained from familiar spirits, and NOT from the Spirit of Yahweh. This is "witchcraft." The power of witchcraft is derived from Satan himself and every attempt at manipulation or control "sells out" more to Satan and strengthens the deception the Jezebel spirit is under.

She will even use prayer to manipulate the one she is attempting to control, especially audible prayed over that person to create the illusion, that doing Jezebel's will is actually "obeying Yahweh," or to generate fear or other emotion within the person which the Jezebel can then use for manipulation of them.

Wants Power

Those who have the Jezebel spirit are attracted to people of power like "moths to flames." Often, a very intelligent, efficient, attractive, and even blatant Jezebel spirit can be found serving "at the feet" of prominent leaders, even in the church. The deception and/or seduction of the Jezebel spirit is often so successful that the leader does not recognize who is at his right hand. The Jezebel's true desire is to gain the power from the person being served. If that person is prophetic in nature, the actual mission is to destroy them by any means available (destroy their credibility, undermine their authority, discredit their ministry, cause them to fall into sexual temptation, etc.).

Ambitious

Those that have the Jezebel spirit are desirous of "moving up the ladder" wherever they are, not that ambition is always "evil." It's just another character trait to look for.

However, you simply will not find a humble, repentant, democratic and non-ambitious person who has the Jezebel spirit.

Convinced

While those who have the Jezebel spirit have a belief system that is obviously incorrect and evil, they are very firmly held beliefs.

Those with the Jezebel spirit are usually people of deep convictions. Many people controlled by the Jezebel spirit have a true heart for God and earnestly desire to serve Him. The original Jezebel spirit was devoutly religious, but was at total enmity (hostile) with God. She worshipped at the altar of Baal (worship of the flesh). Modern day Jezebel spirits may indeed believe they are serving the one true Mighty One/God; however, the true hidden agenda is "self-worship." In many cases they have a Private Interpretation on the Bible, but they will vehemently insist they are correct.

Murmuring, Complaint, and Criticism

Murmuring and complaint and criticism a type of spirit very popular everywhere, especially in the church, which one of the spirits most used by the evil one. She uses criticism of perceived faults in others to build up her own self-esteem, and to justify her disobedience of, or lack of respect for, others. Because she tends to perfectionism, any fault she finds in others is grounds for disobeying their authority. She uses criticism as a tool to manipulate those around her, and along with murmuring and complaint, causes disagreement to weaken her opposition, thereby to gain control over, and to destroy them.

Lustful

Those with the Jezebel spirit have "lustful spirits" with lust for power being primary; their lust may be manifested sexually, if it will bring the desired result. The manifestation varies from a wife withholding sexual union from the husband for manipulative purposes, to utilizing sexual temptation to draw one more powerful into a compromised position that will cause their destruction or downfall.

The Jezebel spirit displays angry, vicious and sometimes violent behavior when opposed. She will turn on the one who refuses to do her will or submit to her (especially if she has been successful in manipulating this person in the past), frequently with a vicious, berating verbal attack aimed at humiliation. The emotional damage caused by these outbreaks can be devastating to the one at whom she directs her wrath. This is often the source of terrible emotional wounds for her children and spouse. When this angry behavior happens in public, it often exposes the true spirit in operation to others who may have been previously deceived. Watch for it.

Infirmities and Disease

The Jezebel spirit frequently enjoy people's poor health, especially the "Low-profile" type. For them, it is a tool for attention, sympathy and other forms of manipulation. The tragedy is that this form of "invited infirmity" eventually leads to real physical problems, and becomes a part of the destruction wrought/worked on the host by this evil spirit, but it serves to further Jezebel's ends, not to weaken her.

Have you ever felt insecure? Be careful, those with the Jezebel spirit love to investigate in the realm of insecurity. She will spot this in you "instantly" and then the seduction begins.

Destruction

In addition to destroying those around her, the Jezebel spirit especially hates the prey she is controlling (remember the mission of the Jezebel spirit is to kill the prophets: the victim is often herself anointed of God to be prophetic), and will ultimately cause her victim to self-destruct. This is referred to as the In the spirit realm, there are two applications:

1. The Jezebel spirit seeks to kill the male authority figures (or prophets) and

2. She seeks to kill her victim, which is mated to her when the Jezebel spirit takes control of their life.

Cursing

Those with the Jezebel spirit curse everyone, unwittingly bringing a curse upon themselves, most of the time. Criticism is a form of cursing, both of the person being criticized, and of God their Maker. Murmuring and complaint is a cursing of circumstances, which also curses God for allowing them. The Jezebel spirit is a master of criticism, murmuring and complaining, as mentioned previously. Often those whom she is at enmity (hostile) with are deliberately cursed in a conscious effort to "punish" and "bring them back into line" to bring them back under her control. The Jezebel spirit firmly believes she has right on her side in doing these things, and displays vicious and callous disregard for the well-being and independence of others, having convinced herself that it is ultimately for their good as well and that she knows best and really has their best interests at heart in doing so. Those people who have been on the receiving side of the Jezebel spirit have felt the curses, anger and viciousness of those curses and many surrender to them. However, for those under the "protection of the Stake/Cross", these curses are most often transformed into blessings instead, leaving the Jezebel spirit sapped of emotional energy, frustrated, confused and completely defeated; wondering what went wrong?

Superiority Complex

The Jezebel spirit frequently perceives themselves as intellectually and spiritually superior to others, and "talk down" to others. This attitude is actually despising of others.

The Jezebel spirit absolutely hates and shuns Repentance and Humility.

Because the Jezebel spirit is prideful and rebellious, she hates repentance and humility. These are two mighty weapons, which can be used against her. This is also the key in discerning this spirit---a pride-filled rebellious person refusing to repent.

Jezebel and Fashion

The Jezebel spirit is very much attracted to the latest fashion in dressing and she dresses up to demonstrate superiority and literally to "kill."

Bitterness and Resentment

Bitterness and resentment against past hurts and offences are nurtured in the victim by the Jezebel spirit, because she knows a root of bitterness will grow like a cancer and manifest itself in all sorts of physical ailments, which she can use as tools of manipulation, as noted above. Of course, this cancer of bitterness is also slowly destroying the victim. In many cases, the countenance of the victim gradually grows more and more unattractive, and in the end, victims controlled by the Jezebel spirit may resemble the very witch like crones often used to symbolize witchcraft---where this spirit is birthed. The victim rots from the inside out, physically and spiritually, and it shows. People eventually find that Jezebel's spirit is "Spiritual ugliness" and very repulsive.

Jezebel Covens

Many with the Jezebel spirit will be drawn to the most influential Jezebel spirit in operation. Though this is done unconsciously, it has the effect of creating a fully-fledged and very effective witches' coven, with a "high priestess" in charge with devastating results! You can see them spread all over the country in the Feministic organizations.

Jezebel and Children

Those with the Jezebel spirit view children as being perverted. She says she loves them, but she really doesn't even know how to love them, using them as weapons to advance her own selfish needs. Children are simply pawns in her power and control games. Indeed the trend now all over the Western world is to have very few children, if any. A Jezebel spirit Feminist said: "The most merciful thing a large family can do to one of its infant members is to kill it."

Jezebel spirit is a classic "Back-stabber:"

She will smile at you, give you a hug and a kiss and then, as soon as you turn-around, stab you in the back, repeatedly, with vigor, enjoying every wound she inflicts. She is a most vicious and devious spirit. Beware.

The above characteristics of the Jezebel spirit are very disturbing. This evil spirit comes from the pits of hell and we need to be aware of those whom cross our paths to steer clear of them as much as possible. We do not want to succumb to the evil Jezebel spirit.

The Spirit of Ahab

One thing to be noted in these days is that in general there are more women in church than men. This occurs when the "spiritual and natural" head of the family is the women. Men have the tendency to "run to the hills" when women infringe upon their roles.

The spirit of Ahab is a weak and emasculated (a man who has been rendered non-effective, or his authority stripped of him) figure, indeed the majority of modern men are under that spirit, enslaved to their women. There is an adage (a traditional saying that expresses something considered to be a general truth) that says: "There are two kinds of people in this world: those who rule and those that are ruled, if you do not rule you are ruled."

It is this Jezebel spirit that comes across as being more spiritual, it is her that takes the leading role, Jezebel used Ahab's emotional stresses to endear herself to him, it was this woman that drove her husband to do what she wanted, she was ruling the roost in every aspect. Is not that a picture of our Democratic culture today?

I'm all in favor of women coming forth in this hour but one of the signs of Jezebel is the next thing I'm talking about is real.

What happens when the woman takes the leading role that God has clearly prescribed for men?

- If a woman plays her husband's role in directing the family, he will lose his natural drive to bear responsibility.
- When a woman takes the lead, she is playing the masculine role. Unless her husband fights her for supremacy, he must assume second place. Men who are forced into subjection to their wives tend to be angry, dejected and retreat like Ahab.
- When a husband steps into a spiritual role at his wife's command, he becomes vulnerable to her guidance in that role. This is against God's

directives and the nature He gave, and often brings conflict in the family and in the church.
- Many men turn their heads when they see their wives stepping out of their God given role. These men would rather not have to deal with the stone-cold anger they would receive from their wives if they offered any resistance. Have you seen that behavior here and there?

Ahab chose not to notice when his wife worked behind the scenes. Many men turn their heads when they see their wives stepping out of their God-given role. Jezebel knew that she was not the rightful head, so she invoked her husband's name to give her word authority. Did you ever hear it said, "Oh, my husband will not let me do that," when you knew in truth he really would not care? It is a way to maintain control and stop those who would question you. When a woman does this, she stops any ministry God has for her.

Jezebel was deeply concerned about spiritual matters and took steps to help promote her spiritual leaders. In the process, she provoked her husband to destroy those in spiritual authority she did not like. Have you ever seen women influencing their husbands to think evil of those in authority because they did not like something about them? When a woman comes to this place, she might as well change her name to "Jezebel."

The fact is that man is made in such a way that he has no defense against the love of a righteous wife, but if he falls into the end of a Jezebel spirit, truly his life will be hell on earth.

Unfortunately for men, with the beginning of Democracy. (a belief that all people are, in principle, equal and should enjoy equal social, political, and economic rights and opportunities) approach there are billions of Jezebel spirits in the world and the once manly men have been reduced to weak types of Ahab's. They have been mentally emasculated and the world is in deep decadence (decay in a society, especially in its morals) because of that, as we see today.

How many women do you actually know do this today?:

> Proverbs 31:10-12 Who can find a virtuous woman? for her price is far above rubies. The heart of her husband doth safely trust in her, so that he shall have no need of spoil. She will do him good and not evil all the days of her life.

For seven years, God had carefully protected Elijah. He fed him in the wilderness. When Ahab's armies sought to kill Elijah, they were unable to lay a single finger on him.

Finally, in a showdown at Mt. Carmel, Elijah called down fire from heaven and resoundingly defeated and killed the priests of Baal. All Israel fell at his feet in repentance, worshipping the true Mighty One/God. Elijah was the man of the hour. He was vindicated, victorious, and clearly in charge.

Nevertheless, when Jezebel sent Elijah a single threat, he suddenly turned coward and fled to the desert. Anxious, depressed, and miserable, he begged God to kill him. Typical of men today, run to the hills.

It makes NO sense. Elijah enjoyed supernatural protection for seven years. He watched fire fall from heaven and defeat his enemies, yet when a single angry woman threatened him one time, he lost every shred of vision and ran away. He moaned in self-pity and depression, begging God to kill him! Surely that was a magnificent display of God's power and that power was with Elijah, but at a word from Jezebel he forgot all that and ran in fear. Surely that must have annoyed God at least a little, for it seems that in that occasion Elijah had more fear of Jezebel than he did of God.

This is a great example of Jezebel's powerful demonic spirit "anointing" to intimidate, create fear, and cause men of God to withdraw. Jezebel' spirit steals our vision. Jezebel' spirit will even make us depressed and anxious when there is nothing significantly different in our circumstances. If there are difficult circumstances, this spirit will tell us they are insurmountable, impossible, and overwhelming. The Jezebel spirit will make us feel like dying that when in reality, we are God's man of the hour.

Jezebel's spirit of witchcraft will attack key leaders in her targeted area through intimidation. Those under attack may awaken one morning to find it takes effort just to breathe. All joy seems to depart. Spiritual life seems irrelevant. Demonic voices will echo in our minds "something's wrong with you!" We may suddenly find ourselves in unreasonable anxiety, fearing tragedy or death. Much of what is called "depression" in the ministry is simply the Jezebel spirit.

The Jezebel spirit wants to paralyze with fear, condemnation, depression, apathy or whatever it takes until we withdraw. The only answer for those under Jezebel's spirit attack is perseverance in battle. We must remain on course no matter how long it takes!

The sad thing is that she is so successful in her endeavor these days.

The war continues today between Jezebel and Elijah. Like all wars, there are casualties. Leaders sometimes fall. Soldiers sometimes withdraw. The Jezebel spirit wants to keep the church and the world within its present boundaries. She claims to decide the extent of the church locally. We must not tolerate this.

We must rid ourselves of Jezebel's ways. We cannot cast out lust when we harbor lust in our lives. We cannot bring down a spirit of control if we use manipulation and hype to control our congregations. We must examine our own ways, and repent of Jezebel.

It takes Jehu. Although Elijah was Jezebel's enemy, it took Jehu to trample Jezebel.

Jehu took no prisoners and showed no mercy to Jezebel. He had singleness of purpose and was driven by it. As he approached Jezebel those who saw his chariot noted he "drives furiously" (2 Kings 9:20). When others offered peace and compromise, Jehu responded "How can there be peace as long as the harlotries and witchcrafts of Jezebel are many?" (2 Kings 9:22)

This is repeated in the New Covenant/Testament:

2 Corinthians 6:15 And what concord hath Christ with Belial? or what part hath he that believeth with an infidel?

Jehu would not rest until Jezebel was dead. Her pleasures could not attract him. Her threats did not deter him. He would not tolerate Jezebel.

Jesus says we too cannot tolerate Jezebel. (Revelation 2:20) We must learn the prophetic power of the word "No!" We must give no ground. Stand FIRM!!!

When Jezebel attempted to captivate Jehu, he did not even allow himself to be drawn into conversation with her. Instead, he called on her eunuchs (a type of today's men) to cast her down from her balcony. Those with the Jehu anointing will call to Jezebel's emasculated slaves to rise up above their miserable situation, and they too will cast her down, and be set free.

"NO" is the operative word against the Jezebel spirit, when those in spiritual authority say "NO" to her, she is ready for war. Remember, Jezebel is a warring spirit who is always dressed for battle.

The time is over nigh, the time is well passed, but we must stand and we must rise up and regain our God given position. What shall we say to our beloved (Christ Jesus), when He will ask us: "What have you done with the life I gave you?" There will be lowering of heads and faint voices: "You know, o Master."

We must all work in one accord with a trowel in one hand a Sword in the other.

> Nehemiah 4:16-18 And it came to pass from that time forth, that the half of my servants wrought in the work, and the other half of them held both the spears, the shields, and the

bows, and the habergeons; and the rulers were behind all the house of Judah. They which builded on the wall, and they that bare burdens, with those that laded, every one with one of his hands wrought in the work, and with the other hand held a weapon. For the builders, every one had his sword girded by his side, and so builded. And he that sounded the trumpet was by me.

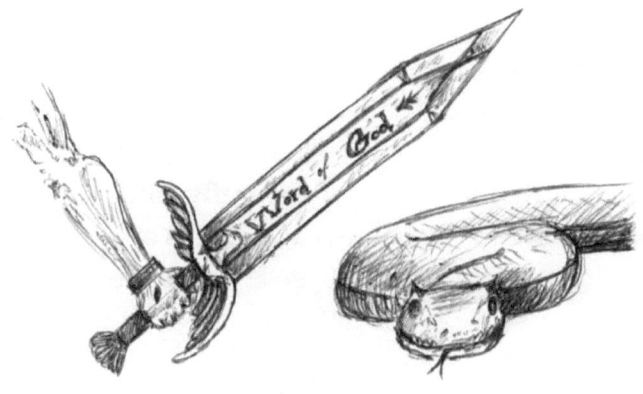

Chapter Four
Network of Demons

Any time you deal with Jezebel you need to realize there are many demons that associate with this spirit. The spirit of **Jezebel** doesn't work alone, she has a network. The **Jezebel** spirit is the most wicked of spirits. Historically, the rise and fall of spiritual power within the Church has been related to the acknowledgement and opposition toward demonic principalities and powers.

You are in a spiritual war whether you want to be or not. There are high level spiritual assignments against you and the Church. One of the most powerful is the Jezebel spirit. That spirit works with a network of demon spirits to steal, kill and destroy your life, marriage, family and ministry. Your success depends on your ability to see this spirit's operations. You can't fight what you can't see. You can see.

Spiritual warfare is part of Christianity and the spiritual warfare is not over. Jesus did not ignore demon powers and he didn't teach his apostles to ignore them either (Matthew 10:1). The Apostle Paul pulled the natural curtain back to see what really goes on in the spiritual realm. He taught the church in Ephesus how to battle unseen spirits saying,

> Ephesians 6:10-13 Finally, my brethren, be strong in the Lord, and in the power of his might. Put on the whole armour of God, that ye may be able to stand against the wiles of the devil. For we wrestle not against flesh and blood, but against principalities, against powers, against the rulers of the darkness of this world, against spiritual wickedness in high places. Wherefore take unto you the whole armour of God, that ye may be able to withstand in the evil day, and having done all, to stand.

Warriors wear armor. Armor is for the fighting man. Like the Apostle Paul you will fight many spiritual battles including those released by the **Jezebel** spirit. As leaders recognize the spiritual warfare released by **Jezebel**'s network of demons they can equip believers to use their delegated spiritual authority to fight back.

> Luke 10:19 Behold, I give unto you power to tread on serpents and scorpions, and over all the power of the enemy: and nothing shall by any means hurt you.

When leaders ignore this dark ruler, believers and the Church suffer. You are not like others. You will not ignore **Jezebel**. You will learn how to stop the **Jezebel** spirit.

The Church has allowed the spirit of Jezebel to run all over the Church. The **Jezebel** spirit is discussed in both the Old Testament and New Testament. Elijah had contact with Queen **Jezebel** and the governing church of Thyatira with a person carrying a **Jezebel** spirit. There are thousands of years between Elijah's face-off and the Thyatira testimony. This gives evidence that the **Jezebel** spirit did not die with a wicked queen.

The church in Thyatira was commanded **not to suffer the spirit of Jezebel**.

> Revelations 2:20 Notwithstanding I have a few things against thee, because thou sufferest that woman Jezebel, which calleth herself a prophetess, to teach and to seduce my servants to commit fornication, and to eat things sacrificed unto idols.

"Sufferest that woman Jezebel" means:

- To allow, permit, and let.
- To allow one to do as he wishes, not to restrain, and to let alone.
- To give up, let go, and leave.

This means you know the **Jezebel** spirit is working through a particular person but refuse to do anything about it. One thing I can tell you for sure, to ignore the Jezebel spirit is ministerial suicide. You cannot beat this devil by leaving it alone. Ignore it and suffer the consequences, confront it and win.

The Jezebel spirit is a "strong man spirit." Strong man spirits watch for gate keepers. Gate keepers control the access to something whether it's wealth, power or influence. A strong man spirit uses other weaker spirits to advance its ambition of dominion. Jesus mentioned strong man spirits saying,

> Mark 3:27 No man can enter into a strong man's house, and spoil his goods, except he will first bind the strong man; and then he will spoil his house.

It's the collective of evil spirits and **Jezebel**'s team that makes the **Jezebel** spirit a strong man spirit. The network consists of many different wicked spirits including whoredom spirits, divination spirits and witchcraft spirits.

The whoredom spirit is part of **Jezebel**'s network of evil spirits. The great sins of **Jezebel** include whoredoms. Jehu mentions the whoredoms and witchcrafts of **Jezebel**.

Chapter Five
Self-Centeredness

One of the most powerful things that can make room for the Jezebel spirit to grow in a person's heart is self-centeredness. Self-centeredness, as opposed to Christ-centeredness, creates in a person:

- a spirit of pride, from which comes an
- unteachable spirit,
- a spirit of control,
- a judgmental spirit and
- a rebellious spirit.

When you meet a person with either of these spirits, look for the others. They will be there. The most obvious one that you have spiritually discerned through the gift of discerning of spirits may overshadow the others. But upon close observation you will see them all in operation. When a person becomes self-centered to the point of pride, and begins to manifest these spirits, it opens up the door for the Jezebel and Ahab spirit, who always bring their idols along with them. With idols always comes sexual immorality, which brings about an abandonment of oneself to fleshly pleasures, drawing the person even further away from God.

The Jezebel spirit will then attempt to play prophet/prophetess by its familiar spirits and really loves a true prophetic gift as long as it edifies, exhorts and comforts. But when a true prophet of God, who has been anointed by God to speak the judgment of God, comes along and exposes this spirit, it attempts to destroy the prophet by:
- Destroying their character.
- Destroying their credibility as a prophetic minister.
- Destroying the conscience of the prophet.

Then the prophet can't differentiate between right and wrong, good and evil, blessing and cursing, or the voice of God and the voice of satan. When a prophet's character and credibility are destroyed then the conscience is ripe for destruction. The prophet is then of no use to God, or to themselves.

At that point Jezebel then declares that true prophet of God that it is attempting to destroy to be a false prophet. Many in the church will agree because they believed the lies about the prophet's character and credibility as a prophetic minister. The prophet him/herself then will begin to doubt their own character and credibility and the inception of the destruction of his/her conscience is established and, without proper prayer and counseling, will continue until the conscience is thoroughly destroyed.

The Jezebel spirit thus establishes itself as a true prophet of God who exposed a false prophet, and draws the engrossed adoration of its followers even further into the slime pit of hell.

That's why discerning of spirits is of such great importance in this day and hour. We will establish the usage of that Holy Spirit gift firmly in our lives by continually remaining and abiding in the presence of the Father.

Chapter Six
Jezebel's Identity

We must understands that not every woman we don't like is indeed Jezebel. We need to be careful not to label someone like she's a Jezebel! We most often attach that familiar phrase and the Old Testament name of Jezebel to women who are seductive in nature with heavily painted faces, or to women who are overly aggressive, controlling and manipulative. While that is not a wholly inaccurate description, the historical Jezebel, who as wife of King Ahab was queen of Israel, was much more than a control freak: Jezebel was inspired by the Deceiver, Satan himself, to establish Phoenician idolatry on a grand scale at her husband's court. To further her cause, she slew the prophets of Jehovah, murdered Naboth for his vineyard and then threatened the life of the prophet Elijah.

Jezebel is also mentioned in the New Testament. Revelation 2:20 describes a Jezebel-type of influence operating in the church of Thyatira. Jesus addressed the church of Thyatira and rebuked it for allowing the woman Jezebel, who called herself a prophetess, to teach and seduce the servants of God. Jezebel's intent in that New Testament church, just as it is today, was to cut off the voice of God's true prophets. Obviously, this cannot be the same identical woman mentioned in the Old Testament who was the queen of Israel; rather, it was the same evil spirit seducing the believers in the church.

We can easily conclude by the mention of Jezebel in both the Old and New Testaments that this evil influence of Satan, operating through a Jezebel-type spirit, lives on and operates even today. This evil spirit continues to seek out individuals, whether male or female (the spirit is non-gender), whom it can influence both in the church and outside the church. The Jezebel spirit works through many different avenues that we will discuss throughout this book. For now, understand that control and manipulation are two of its most identifiable characteristics. In the local church, the spirit can be found in both leadership and congregation. In the marketplace, a Jezebel spirit might manifest through a controlling boss or a seductive competitor. At home, the

Jezebel spirit can operate not only through a husband or wife, but also through a controlling child.

Another recognizable characteristic is false prophecy—remember that Jezebel called herself a "prophetess." We have all been affected by false prophecy through Jezebel's deceptions and the lies of the Deceiver.

The Jezebel spirit attempts to deceive you into believing that you do not belong or that others are continually rejecting you. All of us are confronted by her at one time or another.

Have you been experiencing chronic dissatisfaction? By this I mean, have you sought joy and feel as if you have it, but later realize it was merely a fleeting sense of happiness? Are you frustrated with your life and yourself? At times, do you truly believe that you will never feel loved and accepted? Again, if so, it is very possible that you have been deceived into believing that you cannot trust God for your total fulfillment. You may even be trusting in counterfeit gods without realizing it. The Jezebel spirit is a strong promoter of idolatry.

It is possible that you have been so influenced by the Jezebel spirit that your life feels as if it is spinning out of control. Or you might have awakened one morning and faced the fact that your life is in chaos. Chaos is a word used to describe utter confusion and complete disorder. Spiritually, we know that God is not the author of confusion; the enemy is. When a Jezebel spirit is in operation in our lives, we will most likely experience chaos, confusion and disorder. It is possible in this instance that the spirit of lawlessness may also be in effect.

We cannot allow any spirit of deception, especially Jezebel, to remain in control of our lives. Many have heard me say, "If you ask the devil to dinner, he brings a suitcase." It is true! I know this firsthand. I thank God for the blood of Jesus that cleanses me, and for His power over any demonic influence that tries to control my behavior.

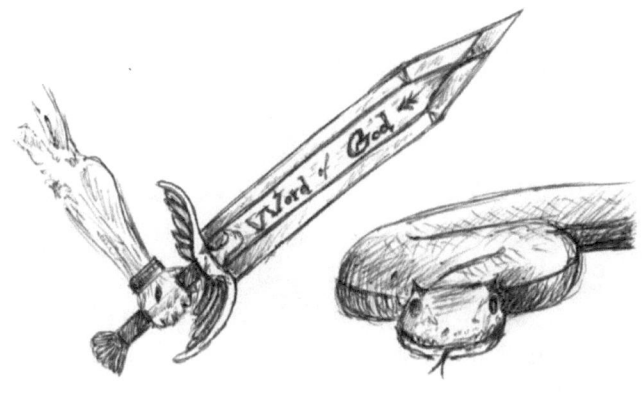

Chapter Seven

Knowing Jezebel

Have you ever heard the saying keep your friends close but keep your enemies closer? I'm not saying we need to be close to Jezebel but we do need to know all we can about this spirit. As the "End Times" are coming closer, I believe the secular, as well as the Christian world, is experiencing a worldwide cleansing. Everywhere sin is being exposed like never before, and God is giving His people divine wisdom to deal with the exposures in His mercy and grace, leading people to God's heart and destiny for their lives, instead of condemning them and leaving them for the world to devour. As the Bride of Christ is becoming whiter, we are also seeing an uprising of the counterfeit spirituality, the seducing spirit of Jezebel, working more actively than ever to kill, steal, and destroy.

While some Christians are ignorant and even skeptical of the spirit of Jezebel, many Christians have become educated in some facets of what this spirit of Jezebel is all about. Even so, many times I get this question when we teach on this subject: "I know I must fight the spirit of Jezebel in the Spirit and not in the flesh, but what exactly does that mean for me in real life? How should I behave around people in my family, my work place, my church etc. who have the spirit of Jezebel?" Many say things like: "I just don't understand why this is happening to me? Why are they doing this to me? I have tried to stand strong and pray but my energy is zapped, and I'm about to give up. Will I ever win over this spirit?"

> Revelations 2:19-25 I know thy works, and charity, and service, and faith, and thy patience, and thy works; and the last to be more than the first. Notwithstanding I have a few things against thee, because thou sufferest that woman Jezebel, which calleth herself a prophetess, to teach and to seduce my servants to commit fornication, and to eat things sacrificed unto idols. And I gave her space to repent of her fornication; and she repented not. Behold, I will cast her into a bed, and them that commit adultery with her into great tribulation, except they repent of their deeds. And I will kill her children with death; and all the churches shall know that I am he which searcheth the reins and hearts: and I will give unto every one of you according to your works. But unto you I say, and unto the rest in Thyatira, as many as have not this doctrine, and which have not known the depths of Satan, as they speak; I will put upon you none other burden. But that which ye have already hold fast till I come.

Jesus is calling Jezebel a false teacher that leads His servants astray, someone who encourage believers to worship idols, eat food offered to idols, and commit sexual sin. (Note that this encouragement can also come in a subtle form, such as an entrapment for you to fall.) You can find Jezebel in any level of society. She can be in your family, your school, work place, church—virtually anywhere. She can be a woman (or a man) who claims to have religious zeal and she calls herself a prophet, and likes to mingle in with the influential people especially in church. This type of person is especially dangerous because it will deceive people to believe she is one of them, and thereby gain their confidence in order to start teaching them "deeper truths" that twist the original Word of God. Some people get so confused by her deep "wisdom" and somehow become addicted to mystifying the Word of God, making it puzzling and withheld to only the "chosen" or "special" one's who are able to understand these truths, that are actually myths. Jezebel's specialty is to ensnare and convince people to follow her teaching's that will lead them to rebellion against God. In their naïveté, people fall for her charm, and give in to idol worship in their lives, just like King Ahab did when he married Jezebel.

> 1 Kings 16:31 And it came to pass, as if it had been a light thing for him to walk in the sins of Jeroboam the son of Nebat, that he took to wife Jezebel the daughter of Ethbaal king of the Zidonians, and went and served Baal, and worshipped him.
>
> 1 Kings 21:25, 26 But there was none like unto Ahab, which did sell himself to work wickedness in the sight of the LORD, whom Jezebel his wife stirred up. And he did very abominably in following idols, according to all things as did the Amorites, whom the LORD cast out before the children of Israel.

The Old Testament's Queen Jezebel of Israel was a worshipper of Baal, a false god who required even human sacrifices, and she encouraged and led others to do the same. This way, she steered the people of Israel onto a path of disobedience toward their true God, and brought evil and destruction into the land. She was able to do this, because of the influence she gained over her husband.

One of the Jezebel spirit's biggest goals is to kill the true prophets of God. An example of this was the prophet Elijah, who, after challenging and killing more than 400 of Queen Jezebel's false Baal prophets, ran out in the desert in panic, after receiving a letter from Jezebel, swearing that she would retaliate and kill him. He was so intimidated by it that he wanted to lay down and die. But Jezebel's predictions were false, as this spirit's many prophesies usually are, and Elijah did not die. God's plan is higher and more powerful than Jezebel's curses.

Let us take a deeper look at the character traits that goes along with the spirit of Jezebel, because it is much more than what meets the eye, and can be extremely difficult to discern for the untrained eye. There are certain characteristics that always seem to follow these women (and men), and we have mapped some of them for you, so you will be able to recognize them in your family, job, school or church, or anywhere else you go. You can only spot the Jezebel spirit when you understand her personality traits, so let's spend some time under her skin.

The very first, and probably most outstanding quality of a person with a Jezebel Spirit, is their undeniable, ever-present need to always be right! They are not humble people who seek the input of others, but have an unquenchable desire to "win" you over in everything.

Another is the "chameleon" Spirit she possesses that allows her to appear a certain way, but not actually be that way. She will adapt to her surroundings to seem like a loving, charming, and even peaceful person, all the while trying to get a hold of your soul. She will appear to blend in, and suddenly, out of nowhere, stick her tongue out, and swallow you up, by verbally attacking you. The Jezebel spirit is born out of witchcraft and is designed to destroy the host (which is the body it lives in), the spouse, children, family, relationships, marriages, the church, the prophets of God, and the body of Christ in general, in every crafty and subtle way possible.

Another aspect is her use of seduction, deception, and manipulation to control your mind, your actions, and your destiny. She wants to see how far she can involve herself into your life, how far you are willing to allow her to go.

Jezebel's usually come in two categories; the active, and the passive. Or as is has been said; the high-profile, and the low-profile. The high-profile, active Jezebel is the woman who is the leader of the home, including everyone in it. She is the one who "wears the pants" in the marriage/family, the overbearing, bossy, in-control, in charge, dominating woman, who is outspoken, bold, and aggressive. The low-profile, passive Jezebel is the woman who controls the husband and family "behind the scenes". She has a meek exterior, and no one would guess that she has the family in a head-lock, quietly controlling, manipulating, and destroying people's lives. She is soft-spoken, seeming submissive and nice on the outside, and only the closest family knows the truth about who she really is.

Jezebel hates children, especially her own, but it takes great discernment to discover it. Women with the Jezebel Spirit tend to treat their children cold and distant, rarely showing tears or emotion. She likes to make sure they don't get any sympathy, because she hates weakness. She doesn't show much love or affection – genuine hugs, smiles, and affirmation are a rare gift. Usually, her children are merely treated as pawns in her game of control and achievement of power. She uses conditional love to ensure her children's subordination. In this way, they will always strive for her attention and approval, and she will glory in it, only for her own self-gratification.

Jezebel will often mix religious terms and phrases to appear godly, but her life doesn't produce godliness. Following her life and example will lead to rebellion, darkness, anger, and strife.

You will many times find a Jezebel woman involved in various types of teaching activities; not only in religious settings, but also places such as schools and in various types of counseling. The reason for this is their need to be an influence to people. The spirit within them drives them to want to reproduce themselves and their teachings to other people. They like to be highly involved in people's personal lives, getting up close and intimate, making people confide in them. Then she becomes important, needed, and wanted, just the way she likes it. Satan places them specifically in teaching positions so they will impart a distorted and untrue message to people, and cause more spiritual and mental darkness to come upon their lives. People may be in a bad condition when they come to her, but they leave worse off than they came.

She is a master of the "blaming game," and is extremely clever in gaining sympathy for herself by producing convincing arguments for her case, usually portraying herself as fair in her assessments. She will twist and turn information to better fit her, even if it involves lying and crying, anything to make you be the responsible or guilty one.

Jezebel does not truly forgive people who offend her. She keeps track of all past offenses, and she uses them to her advantage when she sees the need for manipulation. Her love is always conditional, making you know of the things that please her, so if you do not comply, she will reject you.

The Spirit of Jezebel also produces sexual imbalance and perversion in the children. I have seen many examples of rebellion and extreme dark and obscure behavior in children and teenagers of mothers who possess the Jezebel Spirit. The family around them doesn't seem to understand why the children choose rebellion instead of becoming "normal" like everyone else, not knowing that it is actually not always a choice of conviction, but rather a direct influence by the distorting spirit of Jezebel operating in the family. The control the children are under causes them not to develop as strong, individual, healthy human beings, but causes perversion and confusion, and sexual immorality. Children of Jezebel's can also fall in the exact opposite category, being overly well-behaved, submissive, pleasing, passive, and shy of conflict. They can be recognized by their fear, lack of ambition and self-esteem, many times rather wanting to take the blame for everything upon themselves, instead of searching for justice.

A Jezebel spirit will never admit any fault or wrongdoing. If you plan to confront the Jezebelite with something, you can be totally clear about your problems, and your list of concerns, and yet come out on the other end, totally convinced that you were the only one at fault. The mighty dark cloud of confusion that surrounds the Spirit of Jezebel makes you give up, and give in to her demands without proper reason. You don't even know what hit you, you just don't have the strength to fight her, and you may even feel a sense of relief for achieving peace with her, not realizing the prize you are paying is compromising for the sake of peace.

The spirit of Jezebel brings about a tremendously powerful confusion that can make you doubt everything you stand for. After your first few confrontations, you learn to stay away from coming even remotely close to suggesting correction. You find out, that you are not strong enough to stand up against it, and start becoming passive. This kind of passivity is what King Ahab suffered from, when he looked the other way, instead of confronting the wrong his wife, Queen Jezebel was doing:

> 1 Kings 21:15, 16 And it came to pass, when Jezebel heard that Naboth was stoned, and was dead, that Jezebel said to Ahab, Arise, take possession of the vineyard of Naboth the Jezreelite, which he refused to give thee for money: for Naboth is not alive, but dead. And it came to pass, when Ahab heard that Naboth was dead, that Ahab rose up to go down to the vineyard of Naboth the Jezreelite, to take possession of it.

Because of King Ahab's passive negligence of Queen Jezebel's wicked actions, we have the term "Spirit of Ahab" which is the "perfect" counterpart to Jezebel. He wants to remain innocent, but is anything but innocent in the eyes of God. In fact the Bible says Ahab was an evil man, possessing the same persecuting spirit as his wife, as he mocked the prophet Elijah and called him intimidating names:

> 1 Kings 18:17 And it came to pass, when Ahab saw Elijah, that Ahab said unto him, Art thou he that troubleth Israel?

> 2 Kings 9:31 And as Jehu entered in at the gate, she said, Had Zimri peace, who slew his master?

Remember, Ahab's passivity cost him everything. The Bible says he sold himself to evil. In other words, it's not only through "old-fashion" Satan worship we can sell our souls, but also, when we sell our souls to worship another human being, who will drag us into a life away from God.

> 1 Kings 21:25 But there was none like unto Ahab, which did sell himself to work wickedness in the sight of the LORD, whom Jezebel his wife stirred up.

I believe, we have to understand, that dealing with the Jezebel spirit, will never be peaceful! One has to give, and that is certainly not going to be Jezebel if she has her way. A Jezebelite doesn't respect anyone, and certainly not someone of lesser authority than herself. She will never humble herself and help find a way to make things work. Things have to be her way, or no way at all. King Jehu, the warrior, knew that there is no achieving peace, no compromise that can be made with Jezebel, only a violent counter-action can stop her:

> 2 Kings 9:22 And it came to pass, when Joram saw Jehu, that he said, Is it peace, Jehu? And he answered, What

peace, so long as the whoredoms of thy mother Jezebel and her witchcrafts are so many?

In order to fight Jezebel you have to first come to her level of competition. This means, you have to be as strong and fierce as she is. The Spirit of Jezebel is a very overwhelming and overbearing spirit that gives the Jezebelite an arrogant and self-confident flare and attitude, making her believe she is invincible. She believes with all her might that she is the victim of every seemingly injustice committed against her up through her life, and she is fully convinced that anyone who doesn't buck to her authority, is against her, plotting her downfall. In many cases, the Jezebelite has been the victim of sexual abuse in her childhood, and carries a huge grudge against men, and people in general. So, in order to combat her, you need to first be completely convinced in your belief about what you are dealing with.

You have to know beyond a shadow of a doubt that you are in fact dealing with the spirit of Jezebel in that person. If you doubt your position, Jezebel will for sure chew you up and spit you out. She is strong, manipulative, and very powerful in her witchcraft. She immediately knows it if you are insecure and afraid. Like a predator, her instinct will tell her about the level of your strength and authority. If you are not strong, you will be eaten for breakfast.

You have to be prepared to fight. Fighting could involve relentless letter writing, phone calls, and open communication with spiritual leaders to let her know, that you know what she is up to, and that you are telling the world! What Jezebel fears and hates the most, is when they are exposed. They are usually able to easily seduce and deceive people, so when you expose them, it hits them like a train. They lose their power and get knocked out of their path. In this momentum you can work. That is the time to keep pounding to expose her, because she is weary, and has been taken off guard.

This is where the level of competition is so important. If you are not strongly convinced that you are fighting the spirit of Jezebel, you will not use your tools efficiently. Remember how strongly she is convinced, and match that!

There are some controversial points to the fight against Jezebel that every believer should be aware of: When it comes to Jezebel, you can forget about praying for her to come to truth and repentance. You will be wasting your precious time. Also, you must never sympathize with her. You must be 100% against her, and stop having hopes for her recovery and well-being! She is not your sister or brother in the Lord. She is living in the strength of demonic soul power, absolutely sold out to doing evil, and completely out of the will of God and obedience to God. She is her own master, and ultimately she serves Satan. Yes, you are dealing with a human being behind the Jezebel spirit, but don't be weak. This is a pure spiritual battle. You might ask: "Isn't she just a poor deceived person herself?" Yes, she is deceived, but don't you also be deceived to have any weakness for this person. If you love the person, cut soul ties immediately, and surrender her completely to God, for Him to determine her destiny. Remember again the book of Revelation where God gives her time to repent, but she refuses to do so. Do not try to save her, or you will go down with her. You need to alienate yourself completely, and have no patience and tolerance for her actions.

All these seemingly controversial points for a typical Christian mindset need to be dealt with before you are ready to fight Jezebel. Anything less than these attitudes will cause you to doubt, and fall prey to her. Remember she is ready to devour you, using all kinds of evil, such as confusion, guilt, accusation, and intimidation, among many other things. Don't set out to confront her, and then pull back in the middle of it. She will bite you, and make sure you never gather the courage to combat her again. Her stings are so toxic, they can drive you to a breaking point, even causing you to commit suicide. So do not underestimate what you are dealing with.

Also, do not mock her or hint to her. Do not use sarcasm or irony. Do not let her drag you into an argument, but stay in the Spirit when talking to her. Combating, is not antagonizing or challenging or provoking the spirit in a cynical way, but rather staying on top of her, continuing to expose her unbiblical behavior!

Never tell her any personal things, what you are going through, how you are feeling, or where you are with the Lord. She will suck your information in, and use it against you, by twisting and turning your words, making you feel guilty or defeated, especially in your walk with God. For instance she will say that you are not praying or fasting enough. When she accuses you, do not stay silent and prayerful. Instead, rebuttle everything she says! Be stronger than her. Although she claims to be spiritual and a woman of God, don't believe her. (Note how she never passes on the glory to Jesus, has a hard time worshiping, and doesn't share about her personal love for Jesus in genuine love and humility!)

Treat her as someone who lives in disobedience. Do not be compassionate towards her, thinking she will submit to the Word of God like you do! She is not a real believer; she is an idol-worshiper, and a great deceiver. If you seek to live a God-fearing life, you have nothing in common with her. She is like King Herod who told the wise men to let him know when they found baby-Jesus, so he could come and worship too. It sounded real, but he only said it so he could find out where Jesus was so he could kill Him.

When dealing with Jezebel you have to be able to believe the worst of the worst and never be naive. You must know that you cannot trust Jezebel for a word she is saying. In fact, if she says one thing, make it a habit to automatically believe the opposite. Never make the mistake of believing she has any good intentions. See, the wise men looking for baby-Jesus, the newborn King and Savior, heard from the Lord what to do. Otherwise, they would have succumbed to Herod's evil intentions, without ever understanding and discerning them.

Pray, and ask the Lord whether you should fast in your battle against Jezebel. Pray to God to help you expose the darkness, but do not pray for Jezebel. You need to focus all your energy on staying on top of your game, and not giving up!

Giving up is a major threat to your success in battling Jezebel! She will wear and tear on your life, and seem like she will never give in. She will exhaust you on every level, until all you want to do is quit! No, she will not give in out of herself, but if you stay strong in the Lord, He will make her give in. Usually the battle is long and may take years, but with the right steps to understand your position, you can make it!

Many Jezebels use magic–a kind of witchcraft that doesn't necessarily involve voodoo dolls and animal sacrifices and those kind of things. As the Bible says, she leads the people astray with false teachings. In other words, her magic comes from distorting the things of God: The Word of God, the Spirit of God, prophecies, prayers, healings, miracles, fasting—anything God has given His people to use for worshiping and glorifying God, and living holy lives. That is Jezebel's main domain! For instance, she will not always put needles in dolls, but she will lay hands on you, asking if she can pray for you. Then, she will proceed to speak a false soul-powered prophecy over you, making you focus on a counterfeit spirit of "God" which is not God, but actually the depths of Satan! She sows doubt into your life, so you start looking for answers in the wrong places, and ultimately causes your life to run off track.

Also, be aware that many Jezebels have a demon-empowered telepathic ability! This ability usually works with people they have managed to entice and create a soul tie with! For instance, you may be praying to get out of the darkness and confusion you suddenly find yourself in, and she will be calling you, or she will appear in your thoughts, telling you what to do. Whenever you seek to find God, she will interrupt you by telepathically speaking to your mind, letting you know she is watching you, so you feel trapped and guilty. She is everywhere, demanding your attention. If she gets your attention, she gets your "worship."

I see Jezebel Spirits everywhere manifesting the same ways in different people. It's almost comical how alike they are. The same goes for Jezebel's "victims"; they also talk the same talk no matter where in the world they are. To give you an idea of how a Jezebel victim talks, I will give you some sentences I hear often so you can judge for yourself whether you, or someone you know, has been drinking from Jezebel's poison and eaten the fruits of her false teachings.

Jezebel victims always tend to defend her! They feel responsible to come up for her to let everyone know that she "really is a good person," and that she "really has a good heart and only wants the right things." They say, "she does a lot of good to people," and, "you just have to understand her personality," or, "she doesn't have any bad intentions at all."

What she is actually doing is making her own feelings, opinions, and needs more important than God. The righteous living in God is pushed aside to accommodate her personal perception on the way she sees life. When she lives in fear, controls people, and don't admit any wrong doing, "it's okay," because "nobody's perfect," and "we have to understand where she's coming from and what she has had to battle in her life." Slowly she lifts the focus off God and Jesus and onto herself, making her struggles and shortcomings "understandable" and something we all should sympathize with, instead of suggesting that she should change and repent from wrong and ungodly attitudes.

Although the "victims," as I call it, do not realize or admit that they are afraid of her, you can easily tell how much they actually fear approaching her with anything she doesn't like to hear. They will say to you, "Oh, please don't say anything bad to her. Don't make her upset, or else she will get angry." In other words, they are fearing her reaction and the possible punishment and repercussion they might suffer after trying to speak into her life. They have all tried in the past, and failed miserably at reaching her. Now, they try the approach of being patient and understanding. But no matter their attempts to live in peace, she is never satisfied with them, or what they have to offer. They try to give her everything she wants, whether it be money, things, acknowledgement, encouragement–anything she is demanding. However, no matter their efforts, she will continue to be bitter and hateful to them, be discontent, demand change, demand perfection, throw fits, and demand whatever she wants!

After living with Jezebel for many years, they start becoming weary and disillusioned. They start believing that they really are a failure, as she has been pointing out so clearly, and that they are the one to blame for it all. See the Jezebel Spirit really wants to destroy the person whom carries the demon. The Jezebel Spirit loves to make them suffer internally, digging themselves more and more into the pit of defeat for every day that goes by. The more they try to please her, the more of a sucker they are. And the more she despises them for it. It's like the Devil when he comes to tempt us to fall into sin, and when we finally fall he heaps condemnation on us to make us believe there is no way out for us, although Jesus is willing to forgive any sin. That is the way he traps us in defeat and Jezebel uses the same mechanism.

Be careful who you pray with. Realize that Jezebel grows stronger in their abilities to manipulate, control, and dominate over the years. Some are more seasoned than others, and you will find Jezebels of all levels in churches. Do not intercede with someone who bosses you around, telling you when to pray, and what to pray. Do not pray with someone who stops you to correct your praying by telling you that you are doing it all wrong, and then points out someone else to continue in your place. Do not let her manipulate her way in between you and your other intercessor friends, whom you are in spiritual agreement with, and one with in the Spirit of God, causing a division to come between you, ultimately destroying the prayer group! Do not allow her "take-over" spirit to set the agenda, by running her own mini-ministry inside your prayer group. She will take excess time to read the Word, pray for people un-encouraged, sing or play music way too long, and practice healing and praying as if she is the main minister. It can be difficult to discern the spirits sometimes, but ask the Holy Spirit to expose it. If she starts to run the show, speak up in God's authority! Tell her how you do things according to the order and authority of God's given directions in the Word of God. Do not be afraid of a confrontation, or try to keep the peace with her. If she doesn't submit, ask her to leave! Do not be compassionate with this spirit, as you understand how wicked it is, and how it will drag you and the church down.

Watch out when she starts isolating other prayer partners, spending extra alone time with them. She will often move outside of the building and start leading the group outside, blinding them with "wise teachings" and create soul ties with them. Jezebel works fast and ruthlessly. She goes after the weak one's, and even "buys" them by giving gifts or trips or money, all to get a foot in the door.

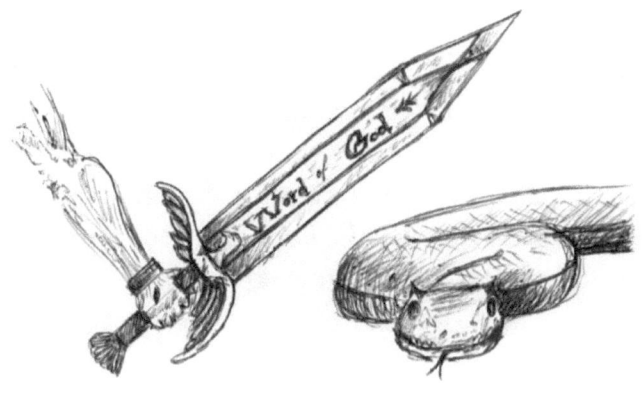

Chapter Eight
God's Covenant

God has been speaking to me about keeping a good covenant with Him in the midst of Jezebel's battle. I wanted to release that here. When contemplating what it means to be yoked, we must always consider it a type of covenant. We are into a covenant, simply by being in agreement. In other words, when we agree with God, we are in covenant with Him. When we agree with Satan (or Jezebel), we are in covenant with him (or her). We can be in covenant, then, with Christ. Or, we can be in covenant with the enemy and be yoked with evil.

A covenant is the strongest form of commitment God can make with mankind. It is a binding contract. One familiar example of this is the covenant God made with Noah, promising that never again would He destroy the earth by covering it with water. His covenant sign was a rainbow, which He placed in the clouds. Each time we notice a rainbow after a rainfall or shower, we may remember God's covenant promise.

The whole of the New Testament is a statement of God's new covenant with us that we can walk in fellowship and new life with Him because of Jesus. Jesus laid down His life to redeem us from sin. He conquered the enemy through His death. Because of His sacrifice, we can enter into covenant relationship by believing and having faith in Him.

> Matthew 11:29, 30 Take my yoke upon you, and learn of me; for I am meek and lowly in heart: and ye shall find rest unto your souls. For my yoke is easy, and my burden is light.

Did you notice that Christ's yoke involves the opposite of oppression and pain? His yoke is good, not harsh or oppressive. Christ offers us rest, relief, ease, refreshment and blessing. His yoke is "comfortable." Now that is a collar worth wearing!

God is a covenant God. Here we will discuss a few basic principles from Elijah's experience that will help you understand God's covenant promises when Jezebel has other plans. God's Covenant at the Brook.

When Elijah gave his prophecy that neither rain nor

dew would fall on the land for the next few years, he was going head to head with King Ahab. Since Ahab was in covenant to an idolater, a controller and a murderer, Elijah was also going toe to toe with Jezebel. It was now Elijah's season of spiritual warfare against the possibility of being in covenant with fear and intimidation

He had just prophesied a drought to this wicked king and queen, but Ahab and Jezebel would not be the only ones affected by this misery. All inhabitants in the land would suffer—including Elijah! Did he know when he prophesied drought that God would take care of his needs? There is no indication scripturally that Elijah was prepared for the drought. But we do know that immediately after he gave the startling prophecy God instructed him to go eastward to Brook Cherith. I imagine Elijah breathed a sigh of relief as he pictured the brook.

Elijah was in covenant with God, and God met his needs. One of God's names is Jehovah Jireh, which means "Jehovah will see or provide." When the Lord sent Elijah to Brook Cherith, He was fulfilling His covenant vow, His promise, to His faithful servant: The name Cherith actually translates as "covenant." Elijah was provided for at Brook Covenant!

We know that Elijah was fed by ravens two times a day—so I suppose God did drop a form of manna from the sky. But, considering that ravens withhold food from their own young, it is miraculous that he actually was brought food by such stingy creatures! This proves the power of obedience when God speaks direction, doesn't it?

From Jezreel, where it is assumed by many that Elijah met Ahab, it is close to twenty miles to Brook Cherith, a journey he probably undertook on foot. Elijah's journey took him through hills, valleys, rocky terrain and mountains. And, again, Elijah was human, a natural man who operated in the supernatural. Since he was a mere man as are we, I believe he was most likely tempted by the enemy in his thoughts. Sometimes when we prophesy against a Jezebel spirit it takes a few days for it to sink in. We wake up one morning thinking, What have I done? This is when we know there will be a counterattack.

Elijah was a prime candidate for fear as he walked alone after having just delivered such an alarming message. I feel sure he looked over his shoulder more than once just to settle it in his heart that he was not being followed by Ahab's army. Yet, we know that Elijah remained steadfast in his journey to Brook Cherith. He held fast to his covenant-keeping God, and, yes, God did provide.

> 1 Kings 17:7-9 And it came to pass after a while, that the brook dried up, because there had been no rain in the land. And the word of the LORD came unto him, saying, Arise, get thee to Zarephath, which belongeth to Zidon, and dwell there: behold, I have commanded a widow woman there to sustain thee.

Often, we have to move forward when we have no idea where provision will come from just as Elijah had to do.

Elijah was so famished when he arrived at Zarephath that he asked a widow who was gathering sticks in the streets to bring him both food and water. He was making this request of a complete stranger who was also experiencing drought and famine—desolation. This poor woman was needy herself Yet she wasted no time, it seems, doing as he asked. She did, however, explain to Elijah her situation:

> 1 Kings 17:12 And she said, As the LORD thy God liveth, I have not a cake, but an handful of meal in a barrel, and a little oil in a cruse: and, behold, I am gathering two sticks, that I may go in and dress it for me and my son, that we may eat it, and die.

When he heard her words, her hopelessness, her place of desolation, Elijah looked upon her with compassion. Any preconceived ideas as to why he was in this city would melt away as he remembered God's mercy. Being in Sidonia, among Baal worship, could have challenged his faith to a certain degree, but Elijah remained in covenant with God and stood on God's covenant. With compassion and divine perception, he prophesied to the widow who was in covenant with fear—which is the bondage of Jezebel.

Elijah said to her, "Don't be afraid. Go home and do as you have said. But first make a small cake of bread for me from what you have and bring it to me, and then make something for yourself and your son. For this is what the Lord, the God of Israel, says: The jar of flour will not be used up and the jug of oil will not run dry until the day the Lord gives rain on the land.

She went away and did as Elijah had told her. So there was food every day for Elijah and for the woman and her family. For the jar of flour was not used up and the jug of oil did not run dry, in keeping with the word of the Lord spoken by Elijah.

> 1 Kings 17:13-16 And Elijah said unto her, Fear not; go and do as thou hast said: but make me thereof a little cake first, and bring it unto me, and after make for thee and for thy son. For thus saith the LORD God of Israel, The barrel of meal shall not waste, neither shall the cruse of oil fail, until the day that the LORD sendeth rain upon the earth. And she went and did according to the saying of Elijah: and she, and he, and her house, did eat many days. And the barrel of meal wasted not, neither did the cruse of oil fail, according to the word of the LORD, which he spake by Elijah.

Elijah's obedience had ended in provision not only for him, but also for others. Isn't that God's heart? His Spirit is continually searching for those who are lost, that He might send "ministers" to them who are obedient and will show His divine mercy.

If we truly are in covenant with God, there is peace, and we experience His divine rest. If we submit to the spirit of Jezebel, the attendant fear and intimidation will provoke us in an ungodly way to attempt to control our circumstances. Control is a form of witchcraft. Control is one of the most obvious signs of one who is affected by a Jezebel spirit.

We know that Jezebel operated in all types of witchcraft. Scripture tells us that a military commander named Jehu was anointed and appointed by God to destroy the house of Ahab and Jezebel. He said these words to Joram, illegitimate king of Israel:

> 2 Kings 9:22 And it came to pass, when Joram saw Jehu, that he said, *Is it* peace, Jehu? And he answered, What peace, so long as the whoredoms of thy mother Jezebel and her witchcrafts *are so* many?

A spirit of Jezebel entrenches a territory with the sin of "witchcrafts" and "fornications."

Fornication is desiring something out of God's timing, and it nullifies the purity of a covenant. Consider the marriage covenant. It is fornication for a man or woman to have sexual union before the covenant of a marriage vow is in place. Similarly, if we get out of God's timing and attempt to manipulate our way into a position of authority within a church setting, this is also a form of fornication—spiritual fornication

Elijah knew how to walk in covenant with God. He knew when to approach Ahab, when to leave Brook Cherith and when to move onto Zarephath He also knew when to prophesy hope to a desolate widow woman. And he knew how to wait.

Elijah is a wonderful example for us to follow as we learn to walk in covenant with God. Sometimes we need to put ourselves in other people's shoes to understand all that they had to press through during their journeys.

Think of how uncomfortable he must have been waiting daily for the ravens to drop food down to him. I can imagine that Elijah's hunger clock was screaming the first few days. Have you noticed that when you miss a meal your stomach suddenly develops a voice of its own? (ravens, like buzzards, are scavengers of carcasses.) Elijah was fed by ravens who brought food from Ahab's table—after all, he and Jezebel may have been the only ones still eating well during the famine.

Patience is truly a virtue. Jezebel wants to seduce us to worry and be fretful and move out from under God's covenant blessings. Many times we do not know how strong we are until we face opposition. Elijah faced hunger and thirst, yet he knew that God wanted him where He had him for a reason. He stayed in covenant, and God was faithful.

Jesus desires to cover you today. His covenant promises are written so that you can receive life. God's Word is fastened with His covenant promises. Imagine a huge net that reaches from Genesis to Revelation—that is our safety net that will catch us when we feel that we have failed God. Romans 8:39 states this concerning God's faithfulness:

> Romans 8:39 Nor height, nor depth, nor any other creature, shall be able to separate us from the love of God, which is in Christ Jesus our Lord.

God's covenant promises are like that huge safety net that is forever there not only to protect us but also to remind us of His mercy. If we have sinned or "fallen," He promises to catch us and then pour out His love and forgiveness. As you move forward in this book I believe the bondage of your past may attempt to clothe you with shame. This is a perfect time to repent for something the Holy Spirit has quickened to your heart. His covenant promises declare that He will never withhold His mercy.

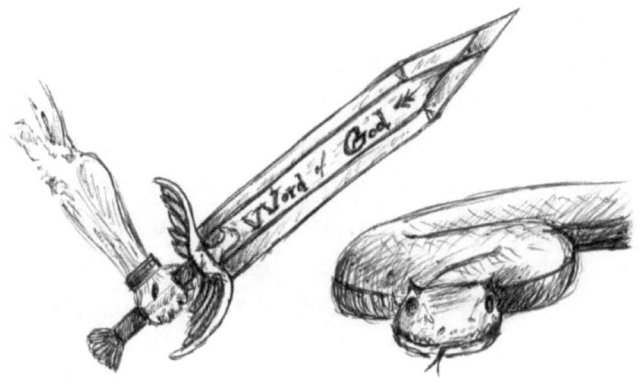

Chapter Nine
Characteristics of Jezebel

I n my book Defeating the Demonic Realm I released several characteristics of Jezebel. I just touched the surface. Here is a more intense list that will help you identify the spirit. Here is the characteristics that accompany the work of the Jezebel spirit. Please keep in mind that a person heavily influenced by this demonic spirit may do many of the following, at one time or another, although not necessarily in the order described. A single characteristic does not indicate that someone has a "full-blown" Jezebel spirit. It may simply mean that the person is still spiritually and emotionally immature. When a combination of several of the characteristics exists, however, there is a strong indication that an individual is influenced by a Jezebel spirit. Also remember that one characteristic may be clearly noticeable, but other traits may be hidden and yet profound. A prolonged manifestation of any of these traits warrants a closer look at the individual and the situation.

While it's almost unrecognizable at first, such individuals are threatened by a prophetic leader, who is the main target of concern. Although such people will seem to have prophetic gifts, their aim is to actually control those who move in the prophetic realm.

To increase their favor, such individuals often zero in on a pastor and church staff, and then seek to find the weakest link in order to subdue them. Their eventual goal is to run the church.

Seeking to gain popular and pastoral endorsement, such individuals will form strategic affiliations with people who are perceived by others to be spiritual or influential with others.

To appear spiritual, such individuals will seek recognition by manipulating situations to gain an advantage. Such individuals often conjure up dreams and visions from their imaginations, or they borrow them from others.

When these individuals receive initial recognition, they often respond with false humility. However, this trait is short-lived.

When confronted, these individuals will become defensive. They will justify their actions with phrases like, "I'm just following God" or "God told me to do this."

These individuals will often allege having great spiritual insight into church government and affairs, but they will not appeal to proper authority rather they first appeal to others. Often their opinion becomes the "last word" on matters, thereby elevating their thoughts above the pastor's.

Having impure motives, these individuals will seek out others, desiring to have "disciples," needing constant affirmation from their followers.

Desiring to avoid accountability, these individuals prefer to pray for people in isolated situations—in a corner or in another room. They use innuendos and false "prophetic" words cannot be easily challenged.

Eager to gain control, these people will gather others and seek to teach them. While the teachings may begin correctly, "doctrine" is often established that is not supported by the Word of God.

Deceiving others by soulish prophecy or by giving words that someone wants to hear, these individuals seek to gain credibility. They prophesy half-truths or little known facts, as though they were from God. Such individuals may also take advantage of someone else's poor memory by twisting their previous prophecies to make it seem as if their words have come to pass.

Although the "laying on of hands" is biblical, these individuals like to impart a higher level in the spirit—or break down walls that have held someone back—by the "laying on of hands." However, their touch is actually a curse. Instead of a holy blessing, an evil spirit may be imparted.

Masking poor self-esteem with spiritual pride, these individuals want to be seen as the most spiritual ones in the church. They may be the first to cry, wail, or mourn — claiming a burden from God. However, they are no different from the Pharisees who announced their gifts in order to be seen by men.

Usually such individual's family life is shaky. These individuals may be single or married. If married, their spouse is usually weak spiritually, unsaved, or miserable. They begin to dominate and control everyone in the family.

The character of the devil does not change, and neither does human nature; therefore, the characteristics of control remain consistent. In various situations, I have observed a number of significant traits that people with a Jezebel spirit display. The traits are amazingly consistent, although the circumstances in which they are displayed may not be even remotely related.

Remember that Jezebel gains a foothold through the flesh, finding access and an open door in a person who has allowed his or her uncrucified flesh and selfish agenda to be in control. A Jezebel spirit is also genderless. It can operate through a man or a woman, and it actively seeks to bring the following traits to the forefront in the person through whom it operates.

- **A Jezebel Refuses to Admit Guilt or Wrongdoing.** The strongest and most evident trait of a person with a Jezebel spirit is that he or she never admits guilt or wrongdoing. To accept responsibility would violate the person's core of insecurity and pride. When a Jezebel apologizes, it is never in true repentance or acknowledgement of wrong. Rather, it is "I'm sorry your feelings were hurt," or "I'm sorry I spoke over your head," or "I'm sorry your face got in front of my fist." You will never hear the person say, "This is totally my fault; I take full responsibility." Always the victim, the person blames everything on someone else. He or she cannot be wrong—ever. When something goes wrong, his or her response might be, "Look what you made me do." If the person admits any guilt, it is twisted around as your fault: "I did steal the money, but it was because you didn't give me enough."

- **Jezebel takes credit for everything.** A person with a Jezebel spirit is quick to take illegitimate credit for accomplishments to which he or she contributed no effort. One spouse might take credit for something the other has done, or an employer might steal the credit for an employee's contribution. Jezebels display boastfulness and pride. In a spiritual setting, a Jezebel's comment might be, "It was my prayer that got results." The person may contribute one idea to a venture and later proclaim he or she did it all: "If it weren't for me, you wouldn't have a church."

- The spirit uses people to accomplish a personal

agenda. Selfishness and greed dominate those with a Jezebel spirit. They let others do their dirty work. A Jezebel will stir up another person's emotions by sowing seeds of division and let that person go into a rage. Then he or she will sit back, looking innocent and say, "Who, me? What did I do?" This behavior makes it difficult for even the most passionate truth seekers to pin a Jezebel down. Skillful at pushing a personal agenda, a Jezebel is difficult to deal with because he or she immediately gets defensive when challenged, attacks you and twists the facts so cleverly that you might walk away feeling confused and even guilty.

- Jezebel withholds information. This trait is a form of control. A Jezebel uses power over you by professing to know something you do not know. In a Jezebel's eyes, having information you lack is a powerful weapon of control. Information is power, so he or she will not offer you any but will attempt to pull information from you. Many of us can identify times when we have had relationships with such people and have found ourselves surrendering personal information to them—knowing as we gave in that the Holy Spirit was telling us to stop. This trait is so strong in Jezebels that you will experience a "pull" from them for information and a surrendering in yourself to give them confidential information. You must make a decision ahead of time not to give in. The majority of the time, the information they seek is none of their business, and they may use it later as ammunition against you.

- The Jezebel Spirit talks in confusion. It is impossible to logically converse with a Jezebel. Keeping things confusing is one way a Jezebel maintains control and domination. Jezebels may change the subject five times in one minute because it keeps them undiscovered and unexposed. They are experts at throwing you into confusion. If you confront them about a specific subject, they will skillfully divert the conversation and take you on a rabbit trail off the subject. This way, they are often able to dodge the truth and remain in charge.

- Jezebel volunteers for anything. Jezebels volunteer in order to establish control. They seem to have endless energy and eagerly look for opportunities to take charge of projects. Although they will work hard, their motive is rarely pure, and eventually their secret agenda of power and control comes out.

- Jezebel lies convincingly. No one can lie better. They turn on the charm and make you believe blue is red. They always fool those whom they have just met, while those they have already victimized stand by helplessly. The fact that a Jezebel can look you in the eye and lie just shows how strong and adamant this rebellious, unruly spirit is. One reason Jezebels are so difficult to pin down is because they have no conscience when it comes to lying. I think that's because their consciences are so seared, they actually believe their own lies.

- Jezebel ignores people. A classic ploy of Jezebels is to ignore you when you disagree with them. Leaders frequently use this tactic when someone does not agree with their plans. They isolate the person by ignoring him, choosing not even to talk to him. Some people are ignored for months just because they choose not to be a puppet and say yes to a controller's every idea or whim. Out of the leader's grace, the person is forced to either "come around" to the leader's way of thinking or be ignored indefinitely. In a controller's mind, no one is free to disagree. Jezebels are also great at using people. When they need you, they quickly warm up to you, but as soon as you have given them what they need, they will ignore you again. When they are done with you, they will throw you away.

- Jezebel never gives credit or shows gratitude. Jezebels will rarely acknowledge another person's actions, not even for something that greatly benefitted them. They just cannot bring themselves to say thank-you or to acknowledge that someone else did something right. This puts controllers in a position of power, and they think that if they acknowledge a gift or kind action, it weakens their power somehow. They also have a sense of entitlement that makes them feel everyone owes them something. A classic Jezebel has the attitude, "You are on this earth to make me happy."

- Jezebel criticizes everyone. Characteristic of Jezebel, controllers always seem to disregard others and hold them in contempt. They have to be the ones who look good, so they sharply criticize anyone else who makes a good suggestion or comes up with a plan. Even if they like a plan, they will criticize it if the idea did not originate with them. Criticizing others elevates controllers in their own minds. They will also show disrespect toward a pastor, a spouse, a boss or even a close friend. They just cannot give compliments—only criticism.

- People with a Jezebel spirit will always upstage others. They brag excessively and are extremely jealous.

Jezebels practice one-upmanship because they feel threatened by anyone who dares to steal their limelight. If you talk about your accomplishments, they will quickly talk about an accomplishment of theirs that is "bigger and brighter" than yours. They will not allow anyone else to upstage them.

- Jezebel seizes information. Jezebels love to control the flow of information. They want to be a walking newspaper. If a situation arises where information is important, they will push to be the first to know all about it. If you talk about an incident, Jezebels will claim that they were already "in the know" and imply that you are a failure somehow. They seem to know everything about everyone. Where they get all their information is beyond comprehension, but they can dictate data and details about people's lives in mass quantities. They relentlessly search for information, even using their children or grandchildren as "spies." You often find yourself spilling your guts to them, even though you know you should not be offering them information. Nor do they respond; they only give you limited bits and pieces. They keep you in the dark because a nondisclosure policy keeps them in control. When you refuse to disclose information, they become angry and moody. But they do not really want to communicate; they only want to dominate and carefully control the conversation.

- Jezebel uses information. Jezebels use information as a leverage for power, perhaps sharing tidbits with you of things told to them in confidence. It gives them a sense of power when they throw you a crumb of information to impress you or gain influence with you.

- Jezebel talks nonstop. Many people talk habitually, but those with a Jezebel spirit talk continually as a form of control. In a typical conversation, they do all the talking, whether it is about sports, the weather or the Kingdom of God. Because of this, they are unable to receive input from anyone else. You have no way of speaking into their lives All conversation with them is one-sided. You do the listening. I have seen Jezebels talk so incessantly that people absolutely cannot get a single word into the conversation. Some controlling ministers will not dialogue with you but will preach at you, as if they are afraid you will say something they cannot agree with.

- Jezebel spiritualizes everything. When controllers are confronted, they commonly spiritualize a situation, explaining it off on God. This prevents them from owning up to any responsibility. Since in their minds God is behind everything they do, their implication is always, "You've got a problem with this; I don't." This leaves you with no recourse—how can you speak into the life of anyone who says "God told me to" about every action they take?

- Jezebel is insubordinate. Jezebels never take the side of an employer, pastor or person in authority unless it will temporarily make them look good. They often will take credit for something they did not do, and they have no conscience when an opportunity for recognition presents itself. But they will not credit or recognize those in authority over them. The bottom line is that they exhibit disrespectfulness and insubordination.

- This Spirit is pushy and domineering. People with a Jezebel spirit pressure you to do things. They seem to rip from you your right to choose or make decisions for yourself. They make you feel as though you do not have enough sense to think for yourself. They will interrupt when you are getting ready to speak into a situation, and they tell you how to think, how to vote, what to eat, how to drive, the best route to take.

- Jezebel operates in clairvoyance and mysticism. Many who operate in a spirit of control also operate in a clairvoyant spirit. The way to discern this is that they have a spirit of pride, not humility. Jezebels have supernatural help sensing information. They may use this against you and say, "I can't tell you how I know this. I just know it." It is not the Holy Spirit behind this, but the help of a clairvoyant or familiar spirit. Clairvoyance is the power to perceive things that are out of the range of human senses. It fools people by looking spiritual. When I have dealt with people who are off track, I have seen this clairvoyance operate. I would open my mouth to speak, and they would preempt me and challenge me on the very subject I was about to address. Astounded, I would be totally caught off guard because they had inside information regarding the very thing I was going to confront them about. In the natural realm, they had no way of knowing what I was going to deal with. They "knew" it supernaturally—by clairvoyance, not by the Holy Spirit. I love and appreciate the prophetic gift of the Holy Spirit, but Jezebels love to operate in this realm illegitimately, through clairvoyance and mysticism.

- Jezebel uses the element of surprise. A large part of a Jezebel's main thrust to be in control involves catching you off guard. The element of surprise works well when Jezebels do things such as showing up a day early for a meeting. It is amazing how they can operate this way time after time under that demonic influence and keep you off guard.

- Jezebel sows seeds of discord. Jezebels will

continually belittle other people in the most subtle ways. Their strategy is to gain control by minimizing another person's value. It is common for them to tell half-truths to implicate another person in your eyes. By sowing these seeds of discord, they hope to eventually reap a harvest of destruction in others' relationships that will improve their position of power.

> Proverbs 6:19 A false witness *that* speaketh lies, and he that soweth discord among brethren.

- Jezebel commands attention. Jezebels like to be the center of attention; they cannot watch others be recognized and praised without becoming jealous and hateful. They exhibit anger about God using and giving favor to someone else. When someone else is recognized, they will quickly undermine the person's accomplishments verbally. The self-centered behavior of Jezebels is self-exalting, and anyone demanding attention becomes their enemy.
- Jezebel is vengeful. Since Jezebels are never wrong, if you contradict or confront them, get ready to become their worst enemy. As long as you agree with them, all is well. But if you challenge them, look out! You become the target of their fiercest venom. They will stop at nothing to destroy your reputation. Amazingly, when you disagree with or frustrate a Jezebel "close friend" who you thought really loved you, he or she is suddenly on a path to destroy you. Because you speak the truth, such Jezebels become vengeful, and you realize their "love" for you was really selfish, manipulative and possessive.
- Jezebel attempts to make others look like the Jezebel. A person with a Jezebel spirit is difficult to pin down. When confronted, a Jezebel will skillfully twist the entire

situation, trying to make the innocent person look like the one attempting to gain control. As always, Jezebels will do anything to look as if they are in the right. In fact, they will twist things around, distort facts and make you out to be the Jezebel.

- Jezebel insinuates disapproval. A Jezebel will often imply disapproval to those under his or her control. The controlled person feels no freedom to express an opinion for fear of disapproval, which often comes in the form of intimidation. This frequently manifests in marriage or in a working environment. Because of your experience with a Jezebel's past behavior, you fear the consequences of expressing your opinion.

- Jezebel knows it all. Jezebels are never shy about letting you know that they are experts on most any subject. They are quick to express their opinions on anything and leave little room for anyone to point out the other side of an issue. Jezebels make idols of their opinions.

- Jezebel is ambitious. A Jezebel has a strong desire, but all for self. "I want what I want when I want it" describes his or her worship of self-will. Jezebel leaders will never use the words, "We have a vision," but rather, "My vision is thus-and-so." They think the universe centers around them, and the vision has to be their idea.

- Jezebel is about gift giving. Naturally, not everyone who gives gifts is guilty of having controlling motives, but gift giving is one tactic used by those who need to control others. Jezebels use gift giving as a form of manipulation to make you feel obligated to them. They want you to "owe" them because it compromises your ability to confront them. Jezebels also can use the timing of a gift as a ploy to get you to cooperate with their agenda. Along with the gift, there can be a strong underlying current of "you owe me" or "after all I've done for you . . ." A gift is not a gift if strings are attached.

- Jezebel is independent. No one has input into the lives of Jezebels. They fraternize with no one—unless it is to get someone to "cooperate" with their personal agenda. They are not team players and refuse to share power and position with anyone unless they can control the relationship.

- Jezebel acts religious. Jezebels dwell in the local church but do not respect positions of authority unless they hold them. They are socially conscious but not Kingdom conscious.

- Jezebel hides from true repentance. We all want to believe a person who had a Jezebel spirit is delivered. The person may indeed seem "normal" for a time and stop exhibiting the classic traits I have listed here. Then suddenly, without warning, a situation will arise where once again that spirit is taking control and the person is wreaking havoc in others' lives. True and lasting repentance only comes when those people in the grip of Jezebel turn from living in the flesh and stop opening the door to evil. Only then will they be delivered.

- Jezebel demands forgiveness but does not forgive. Jezebels might mumble something about how they forgive you, but because they want to maintain power, they "save" your offense to use as future ammunition. They do not totally reconcile, but hold a grudge, even though the Bible says love "keeps no record of wrongs" (1 Corinthians 13:5, niv). Jesus was very clear when He said,

> Matthew 6:14, 15 For if ye forgive men their trespasses, your heavenly Father will also forgive you: But if ye forgive not

men their trespasses, neither will your Father forgive your trespasses.

- Jezebels do not forgive because they see themselves as either a victim or as more spiritual than anyone else.
- Jezebel cannot receive correction. Jezebels are so wounded and insecure that they perceive all correction as more rejection. They avoid rejection at all costs and will attack anyone who they perceive is rejecting them. The only thing you can give them is a compliment in a soft tone—if anything else comes out of your mouth; you are "abusive."
- Jezebel exaggerates and dramatizes situations. When dealing with a Jezebel spirit, get ready for exaggeration of the facts and dramatization of the situation. When Jezebels find one person who has an issue with something they also dislike, they will turn it into, "Everyone is saying this . . ." Then they will make the case that you are the only one not in agreement with them, and that you are in the wrong.
- Jezebel love's to play the drama queen. Jezebels are amazingly skilled at creating drama where no crisis exists. When you gently try to bring up a problem, all of a sudden they will create a huge drama, which fills the room with strife and confusion.
- Jezebel puts words in other people's mouths. Jezebels who desire position or influence will put words in other people's mouths to get what they want. They display presumption.
- Jezebel is masterful at projection. Since they cannot be wrong, Jezebels will project blame on you—accusing you of behavior that sounds as if they are describing

themselves. For example, if they are full of pride, they will accuse you of being prideful. Eliab, David's oldest brother, projected his pride and jealousy onto David: "I know your pride and the insolence of your heart, for you have come down to see the battle" (1 Samuel 17:28). And King Ahab called the prophet Elijah the "troubler of Israel," though he himself was the problem (1 Kings 18:17–18).

- Jezebel love's labels and titles. Jezebels love labels and titles that make them look and sound important. They project the illusion of power. In a church setting, many Jezebels insist on being called a prophet or a prophetess. They have no humility and demand recognition.
- Jezebel displays a critical spirit. Jezebels try to keep the upper hand by displaying a consistently critical spirit. If you have a new home or new car, they will make sure to tell you everything negative they can think of about it. If you like something, they will criticize it. If you dislike something, they will compliment it.
- Jezebel loves to vent. Controllers with Jezebel spirits have no problem "losing it" and letting you have it. Then, after they feel better, they act as though nothing has happened—while their victims are looking for a needle and thread to sew their heads back on.
- Jezebel uses self-pity as a hook. Jezebels can sulk and play the martyr better than anyone. "Why are you being so mean to me?" they might ask if you dare disagree with them. When you stand up to them and confront their behaviors, they will become extremely emotional—either with anger and accusations, or with crying and a sad disposition. They may even threaten suicide as a means of gaining sympathy and maintaining their control.

We each have the freedom to make decisions, make mistakes, think for ourselves, communicate, decide on our likes and dislikes, express our tastes and be creative. We have the freedom to walk away from Jezebel and its influence and walk in the ways of God's Spirit.

Controllers operating under the influence of Jezebel are not free. Tightly bound by their self-centeredness, woundedness and need for power and control, they worship their own will and their own way. But we do not have to be bound by our past behaviors. Even someone with a Jezebel spirit can choose to repent and change. Thank God for the freedom to choose differently and to live in freedom, guided by the Holy Spirit instead.

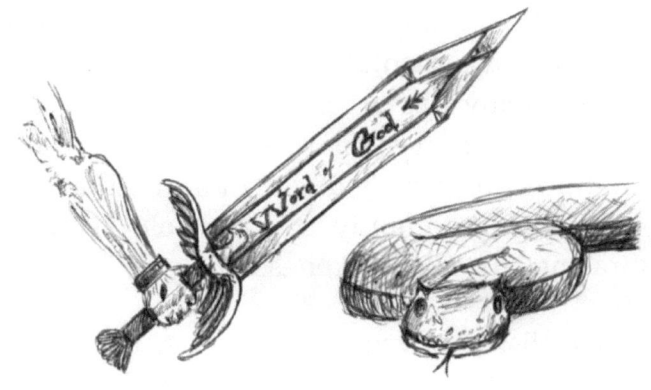

Chapter Ten
Strongholds of Jezebel

We can't really destroy Jezebel unless we destroy it's strongholds. We have to understand this to have victory. stronghold is an area of the mind where darkness reigns. It is a system of logic, rooted in a lie, that an individual has come to accept. This system of thought is formed behind any habitual response, addiction, fixation, compulsion, obsession, and/or excessive fear.

A stronghold is any thought pattern alien to the Word of God. It serves as a mental or emotional "command post" to which the enemy has access. This mental or emotional word or thought system is designed to create misinformation and thereby affect an individual's decision-making ability. Consequently, a stronghold keeps a person from embracing true Christlikeness.

I have listed some important truths about how strongholds operate and hold people captive: around the world and in our lives.

- Strongholds form presuppositions that distort our perceptions of everything we encounter.
- Everyone has strongholds in their lives.
- None of us are as free as Jesus' death on the Cross was purposed to make us. Remember, the blood of Jesus cleanses us from all sin (1 John 1:7). His blood is a weapon that disables strongholds.

STRONGHOLDS IN OPERATION

- Strongholds prevent or retard our emotional and spiritual growth and maturity.
- Strongholds cause conflict, separation, and divorce in marriage. In the church, strongholds cause division. They provoke bitterness, jealousy, anxiety, and depression.
- Strongholds empower Satan and his demons, while grieving the Holy Spirit and God's angels.
- Strongholds keep individuals from accepting what Christ has made them to be and thus keeps

them from fulfilling their personal destiny in God.

- Strongholds are a foothold or a place of operation that the devil possesses in us (Ephesians 4:22).
- Strongholds produce financial disorder and will bring about spiritual disorientation.
- Strongholds weaken our body and make us vulnerable to diseases.
- Strongholds provoke us to respond to others in ways that even I do not understand. They fragment attempted friendships and steal our joy and hope.
- Strongholds stifle our faith and distort Scripture. They cloud and darken our minds and imprison our spirit.
- Strongholds can only be killed at the root. They cannot be removed simply by addressing the manifestation.
- Strongholds allow us to give only a begrudging love, at best. They keep us from forgiving others.

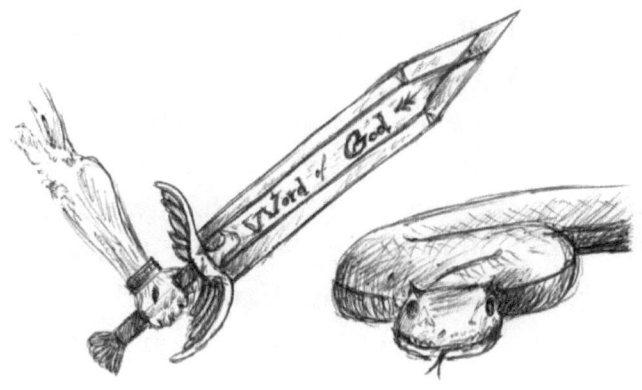

Chapter Eleven
Control of Jezebel

Jezebel always loves to be in control. Two things have always plagued the Church—controllers and their desire to dominate. The power struggle these two bring on has always divided the Church and short-circuited its power. They also plague many family scenarios and can do great damage there, too, especially to children.

The desire to control and dominate, if not mastered, can lead to witchcraft. Witchcraft is nothing more than illegitimately controlling the will of another person. It is a work of the flesh (Galatians 5:19–20) that manifests in three ways—manipulation, intimidation and domination. The desire to control is similar to witchcraft because it stands in total contradiction to the nature of God. He gave the irrevocable gift of free will to all humankind, and He Himself refuses to violate that gift. He will woo us, draw us and attempt to lead us, but He always leaves it up to us to choose His way:

> Deuteronomy 30:19 I call heaven and earth to record this day against you, *that* I have set before you life and death, blessing and cursing: therefore choose life, that both thou and thy seed may live:

The most common way someone with a spirit of control operates is through manipulation. This usually comes across as "If you do this for me, I'll do this for you." Manipulation always has a motive with it. It comes in countless forms such as flattery, self-pity, hinting for something and the like. It begins in simple ways—for example, a child who throws a tantrum to get his own way. He may manipulate his parents in front of other adults by throwing a fit at an opportune time, knowing they will not take action with company present (although they should).

In marriages manipulation takes on another form, usually manifesting through means of the silent treatment, dignified pouting or sulking. The wife may withhold sex or use seductive charms to get what she wants. The husband may withhold finances or employ countless other manipulative actions to get his way. Nothing is more repulsive than a man who puts his wife down, especially in front of others. Men who do this have such poor self-esteem that they belittle their wives to make themselves feel better.

Many spouses have stayed in a destructive marriage because the selfish, manipulative and egoistical husband or wife cries, "If you leave me, I'll kill myself." Not wanting to be responsible for a death, the naïve spouse, yielding to a sickening fear, accepts this form of manipulation and decides to stay in spite of emotional and physical abuse and unprecedented misery.

In the ministry, manipulation is a tool often used to put guilt on people. "Send money to this ministry, or I'm going off the air and the blood will be on your hands." Or, "You must give if you expect God to bless you." Manipulation to extract money comes in many forms, but all manipulation is evil in that it illegitimately controls people. Additionally, it hinders the Holy Spirit from directing people to give money as He moves on them. The principles and blessings of giving fill the entire Bible, but people must have freedom to follow the Holy Spirit regarding where, when and how much to give.

Manipulation is the most common form of control, and Jezebels have learned to use it to get their own way. Some even train their children in it by using manipulative tactics on them such as, "If you don't clean your room, you can't have ice cream." "If you really love me, you'll clean your room." Jezebels are also overprotective and smother their children, not teaching them to interact with others properly. We have created a society of youth who have become master manipulators because they were raised in an environment of control through manipulation.

Parents often give away their authority to their children. They allow the children to usurp their parental authority because they do not want to contend with the warfare they will experience by putting their foot down.

Another way a controller operates is by using intimidation along with fear. Intimidation usually carries with it the threat of losing something, such as, "If you want to keep your job (or remain in this marriage), you must do such and such." Anytime controlling people are unsure of their position or authority, they rely on intimidation. A boss may intimidate employees simply by raising an eyebrow, which implies that if the employees do not go along with the boss's action, there will be consequences.

Intimidation always seeks to move another person through threats. The use of fear keeps the victim under control because he or she is afraid of losing something precious. Intimidators use fear to paralyze people and provoke a specific response. Intimidation and fear are the blatant use of control through the exercise of illegitimate authority.

Another drastic method a controller uses is domination—dominating the will of another person. This is the most dastardly type of control because it leaves the controlled person no option. Husbands use this method over battered wives, not letting them out of their sight or threatening them with injury or death if they attempt to leave.

A person with a dominating personality makes his or

her victims feel suffocated and literally powerless to disagree. Victims feel so controlled by the threat of disapproval, violence or scornful rebuke that they fear speaking up. Dominating controllers usually contradict everything you say. You know that no matter what your statement, they will dispute it. If you say, "It's one o'clock," the controller will say, "No, it's one minute past one." They also continually point out tiny flaws. Their low self-esteem seems to gain a notch by finding imperfections in those around them.

Controllers usually come from the ranks of those who have been controlled and taken advantage of. They learn it through someone doing it to them. Many times a woman who has had a dominating mother will follow the example modeled before her; a man might duplicate the behavior of his controlling father.

Many women abused by men live their lives trying to get back at men because they feel they have been victimized. Living in a male-dominated world, often without real love and protection, they seek to protect themselves by becoming just like the ones they despise. Rather than feel they are being controlled, they learn to control. Their desire is to live in some fashion un-abused and protected from the harshness of men, who have not been gentle and loving in their past. Their woundedness is evident, and they frequently are defensive and cold in their emotions.

Since women are not as physically strong as men, a

controlling female becomes skilled at charms and seductions, temper tantrums and put-downs. Without using physical force, she can learn to position herself to stay in control. In reality, she is submitting to a Jezebel spirit, and her thoughts are structured by it. This woman may not necessarily have a Jezebel spirit at the start, but her way of thinking may help a Jezebel spirit easily find a home. Many women have, to some extent, had this thought structure put on them as they are growing up.

I should point out that if a woman has a strong, bold personality, that does not necessarily make her a Jezebel. People often mistake assertiveness for control, an error in judgment that can be very damaging to this type of woman. Scripture advocates that a woman have a quiet and gentle spirit (see 1 Peter 3:4), but this does not mean she has to be a sweet pushover!

A controlling woman's spirit, in full maturity, is in total rebellion against God. Jezebel tries to turn everything into the opposite of what God intended. This principality so resents men that it ultimately identifies God as the source of putting men "over" women. Basically, it hates all order that God has instituted, and in its full expression, it tries to make men into women. Remember that Queen Jezebel surrounded herself with eunuchs. The Jezebel principality tries to make men into homosexuals. It seeks to turn men into women—feminizing their hair and clothes, getting them to display a lack of masculinity, an effeminate voice and so forth.

A Jezebel spirit comes subtly into a church, often

through a false ministry. A controlling person with a prophetic gift will use it unlawfully to gain a following of people whom he or she can control. Flattery also is used because it plays on the insecurity of others. Although there is flattery in public, there is criticism in private. People with Jezebel spirits seek to tear down others to elevate themselves. Those who love control also love recognition. Seeking recognition and authority, they want to draw people in and subsequently take advantage of them. This process is nothing more than manipulation in order to build a platform to gain control in a church.

True prophetic gifting, on the other hand, operates out of humility and accountability, not control and manipulation. True ministry never labels itself, but lets people discover it on their own. True ministers allow others to "test the spirit" to see if they are of God. If you have a genuine call of God, others will bear witness of you. Do not wear a badge. If you have a prophetic gift, let people recognize it. Do not cheapen yourself by sticking the label on yourself. Pastors sometimes ask me what title I prefer, Prophet, evangelist or teacher? I say simply, "My name is Bill." "Let another man praise you, and not your own mouth" (Proverbs 27:2).

By the same token, why take it so personally if prophetic words or wisdom from God are not recognized or received? Those who take it personally will usually leave (or threaten to leave) a church because their "ministry" is not received by leadership. The Lord revealed to me that if you are upset over how people received your "message," it is an indication that the message came from you and not from God. If it is God's message, He should be the one who is upset, not you. You are not in charge; God is. You and I are free to obey the Lord and leave the results to Him.

Deep insecurity lies at the root of a controlling personality. Insecurity is the deepest root cause of fear, jealousy, anger, resentment, bitterness and a need to be right.

Those plagued with insecurity carry a great sense of rejection and seek attention and approval. The difficulty of insecurity and inferiority comes to a head in the desire to control. Finding feelings of inferiority intolerable, the mentality flip-flops into a sense of superiority and pride. This often occurs in someone who feels his or her physical body does not measure up. This person who once felt so deeply inferior now, in a perverted sense, feels superior to everyone. He or she becomes a know-it-all and is threatened by anyone who dares to disagree, seeing them as the enemy. Extremely opinionated, this person is now quick to express his or her opinion as the final authority. No other input needed, thank you!

The power of control gives insecure people a feeling of self-worth and importance. It validates their existence. Controlling behavior often begins at a young age, especially if a child is not disciplined. Most often, it develops into a lifestyle. That is why it is so rare to see those with a controlling spirit totally delivered. Controlling has become such a part of their nature that it literally becomes part of their personality. And as I said before, some may ask why this kind of damaging spirit, operating in the demonic, cannot be cast out. But simply put, one cannot cast out a personality. That is why repentance is mandatory before the demonic influence can be dealt with.

There is a consistent connection between low self-esteem and a determination to control others. With the feeling of poor self-worth comes such a spirit of rejection that the only way the person perceives that he or she can obtain acceptance, recognition or power is through the vehicle of control. You can almost hear the controller reason, I'm sick of low self-worth and rejection, so I will take control of every person in my path, and no one will ever make me feel this way again.

Here are some motivations behind a controlling personality:

- They cannot bear to be wrong.
- They have a need to be elevated, so they will award themselves credit and even titles. They have a need to feel power and authority, and they will do anything to achieve those. They feel they know more than anyone

Boasting is closely related to pride. Controllers take credit for everything and blame for nothing. Because of insecurity and rejection, controllers feel driven to remind everyone how successful their life is, what great accomplishments their children have attained, and so on. Of course, boasters are not even remotely interested in the achievements of those listening. They are too busy desperately trying to elevate themselves in their own minds.

Controllers are bound with a fear of rejection.

Characteristically, their lives have to be perfect. Therefore, you may observe in them a strong preoccupation with looks, clothes, makeup, jewelry, cars and cleanliness. Controllers cannot bear the thought of being seen in public as less than perfect. They carefully choose their environment so that they will never be perceived by anyone as less than perfect. This, of course, is far from living in freedom.

Controllers also desire to be able to predict things at every stage of life. Seeking predictability leads to control, because controllers manipulate their circumstances so much that they end up attempting to reposition everything in their lives—including both things and people. The less predictable a situation is, the more insecure controllers feel.

Controllers expend great effort manipulating people and circumstances so that nothing is left to chance. A simple change of plans can magnify their insecurity and put them out of sorts. They not only lack trust in God, they are often hostile toward Him. They see Him as the guilty party for not cooperating with their desire for events to unfold predictably.

Not everyone who is insecure is a controlling person. The truth is that we all have a measure of insecurity within us. No doubt it goes all the way back to when Adam and Eve, upon sinning, experienced insecurity and tried to hide from God (Genesis 3). We live in an insecure world. Many of us strive to dress a certain way, to own certain possessions, to attain power and find acceptance—all to fulfill an insecure void within. Criticism is rooted in insecurity. Criticizing others elevates an insecure person in his or her mind. Hearing other people's accomplishments praised usually causes a reaction, making those with insecurities feel fragile and like less of a person. They will quickly say something to upgrade their own accomplishments in view of what has been spoken in praise of someone else.

Insecurity needs to be taken to the cross. The security of every believer is in the person of Jesus Christ. We need to be secure in Christ and let Him deliver us from our insecurities. When we relinquish all rights to our lives and lay them at the foot of the cross, we walk away free!

In Christ we declare our helplessness and receive His acceptance, "to the praise of the glory of His grace, by which He made us accepted in the Beloved" (Ephesians 1:6). His unconditional love defeats all rejection, and we are free in Him. No longer do we perceive His love for us as tied to our performance. His love saturates our being, and we know we are loved and accepted in spite of any flaws or failures.

If we are fearful and need to control the people and circumstances around us, we have not yet received God's love.

> 1 John 4:18 There is no fear in love; but perfect love casteth out fear: because fear hath torment. He that feareth is not made perfect in love.

In a family setting, the controlling parent often dominates the children and places them in the position of siding against the opposing parent. This parent controls the children's line of communication so that the other parent only gets "old news." The passive parent is basically out of the loop unless he or she is urgently needed to solve problems that the controlling parent caused.

If their parents are not on the same page, children learn to manipulate by going through one parent but not dealing directly with the other. They unknowingly violate the Scripture,

> Ephesians 6:2, 3 Honour thy father and mother; (which is the first commandment with promise;) That it may be well with thee, and thou mayest live long on the earth.

Children ultimately resent a passive (Ahab-like) parent for not protecting them in this kind of family scenario. To correct or prevent such issues, the uncontrolling parent must become assertive, asking questions and making individual time with each child, regardless of age, to stay in the loop with his or her life. The passive parent must also become willing to confront the controlling parent without fear of his or her reaction. There will be a reaction, but the children's well-being is worth the price of confronting any issues that are keeping the family from relating on healthier terms.

When insecure people are confronted with truth, they perceive their confronter as the enemy and counterattack. In fact, there seems to be no greater wrath than that of a controlling person who is confronted. This person will forcefully retaliate, never admitting guilt or relinquishing his or her sense of power.

Defensiveness is an insecure person's common reaction even to suggestions. Deeply rooted insecurity cannot take correction, because all correction is perceived as rejection. Therefore, you will never hear an insecure person with a controlling spirit admit to being wrong. It is always someone else's fault. Never is there confession of guilt, contrition or true remorse. If you confront a controller and insist on an apology, you will probably get a screaming response such as, "Yes, I'm wrong! I'm always wrong! I'm a total failure!" This sarcastic spewing is a long way from repentance. The loud volume of the sarcasm is the person's way of telling you, "I'm still in control."

Jesus was in an abusive situation prior Calvary, but in that time He committed Himself to His Father. He chose to entrust His life to the Father's hands, not take things into His own hands,

> 1 Peter 2:23 Who, when he was reviled, reviled not again; when he suffered, he threatened not; but committed *himself* to him that judgeth righteously:

Controllers do not want to leave things to God. They want to bring them to pass on their own. Not trusting God to vindicate them, they seek to control, justifying their actions as "doing it to others, before they do it to me."

The Holy Spirit is our Helper who strengthens us to overcome all obstacles. He teaches us to put our trust in God, not in ourselves, and leave the results to Him:

> 1 Peter 2:6 Wherefore also it is contained in the scripture, Behold, I lay in Sion a chief corner stone, elect, precious: and he that believeth on him shall not be confounded.

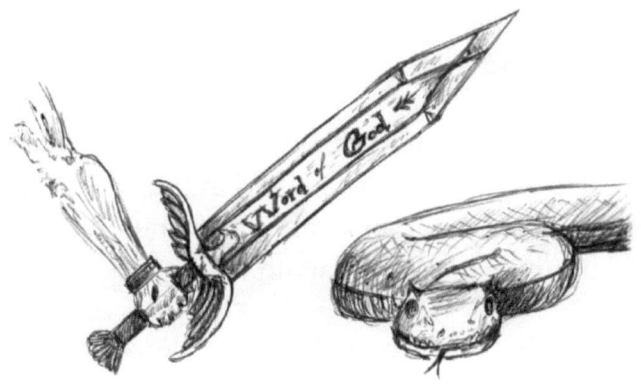

Chapter Twelve

Dealing With Jezebel

I said before that there was going to be a need to repeat myself and here we are. Some of the characteristics will be repeated here for the purpose of dealing with this fowl spirit. In the Bible, Jezebel was a powerful, wicked queen, and wife of a passive king called Ahab. She was a false prophetess who worshiped the false god, Baal. Baal was the god of prosperity, god of the harvests, god of fertility and sex. (Does this sound like some of the modern day gospels that some people preach?)

Child sacrifices were common. Several eunuchs, at the order of Commander Jehu, killed her.

Jezebel was a witch, and her spirit of witchcraft is still in operation today in the church, and in the world. It will take both a Jehu and the cooperation of the injured victims (spiritual eunuchs) to kill her again.

The Jezebel spirit is sociopathic. Behaviors you might see:

- They gain power by destroying others. It is like an adrenalin rush when they "win" over someone. They manage to get in positions of authority, and are difficult to displace, once there.
- They are controlling, manipulative, bossy.
- They can either be war-like in their personalities, so that they are intimidating,

So "sweet," "perfect," deceitful, "timid" and sneaky, they are able to fool and recruit others to join them. Sometimes they can be very charming and charismatic.

- Critical of others, vicious to the point of bloodthirsty.
- They are never wrong.
- They recruit others in their charges against their victims. They act to persuade recruits, and do not give up this activity until the recruits are won over. If the potential recruits do not cooperate and buy into things, this angers them.

- They are narcissic. While they can tend to be oversensitive themselves, they have no concern for the feelings of others. They are not sympathetic to their victims, and tend to play the role of victim themselves, in order to gain sympathy. This way the real victim is left stranded, and opposed by others if they ask for help. Being the center of attention really pleases them.
- They lie, and they believe their own lie. Avoiding the truth, or intentionally acting to withhold truth is part of this. False picture is presented to others.
- Impulsive, failure to plan ahead. Chaotic at times
- Lack of remorse after hurting someone. They justify the harm.
- Consistent irresponsibility.
- Irritability, aggressiveness (open , or subtle), can be quick tempered.
- Failure to conform to social norms. Person is an "outlier" or non-conformist. Has their own ways.
- Psychological counseling will not help, since they deny what they are.
- Claims to religious sentiments, but very superficial in devotion. Born-again status is debatable, and unlikely, but would have to be evaluated on an individual basis.
- Usually women, but can be men. The women tend to control their men with sex. And they pick passive men (Ahabs) so they can dominate them.

- Usually married. If single, could be lesbian, homosexual man, or promiscuous man.
- They falsely accuse you, and they do NOT forgive you …..

How to break this spirit:

Since these individuals usually have achieved some level of authority, only someone who outranks them, or a group effort will work. If you are a woman, you need to strong and self-confident. If you are a man, you need to be the same, and also not be influenced by threats or tears out of a woman. You also need to have enough male hormone to stand up to her. Also, if you are a man, and this is your wife, be sure the men in your support group can be trusted with her.

- Be sure you are not enabling this person; ie. you are not an "Ahab".
- Gather facts about the person's activity and behavior, be able to prove it. you have to start by addressing real behavior. You cannot start by telling someone "they have a spirit." Be prepared to question the person why they behave that way. Make a list of wrongs. Be prepared.
- Gather witnesses, who are also sincere believers (if in a church setting), or other credible authority figures, because the person will attack back, and deny everything. The aggressive types will use their authority to abuse, criticize, and threaten you, and try to have you discredited, or removed. The more sneaky types

go into "victim hood" mode, immediately trying to solicit and recruit support, and make you look like you are the abusive one.
- Isolate the person. Make sure their own recruits (buddies) are not around. It gets its power from others....so if you get it alone, it is more vulnerable, and more easily defeated. You have to remove the source of its power and "gang up" on it.
- Confront the person with the facts. expect denial. They will lie through their teeth!!
- Reject the person's behavior based on the facts. Tell the person they will not be accepted back into the group unless they repent.
- If the person repents – showing willingness to change.
- Church setting – as a group, bind and cast out the demonic spirit in Jesus name, and persist until it is gone. Expect high resistance, since it is a controlling (witch) spirit. There will be screaming and yelling before it is cast out. It will try to attack you and call you names. Also, expect and ignore plays a victim during deliverance. Sometimes the spirit cycles between being the attacker, and being a victim. This is to confuse you, so do not give in.
- Secular setting – document records, give warning that future behavior will be monitored. This is because their basic nature has not changed yet, and an eventual repeat of behavior will occur. If it does, the person needs to be fired.

- Once the spirit is gone, the person needs support and counseling to examine how the spirit entered to begin with, so they can close the door on further attempts by the spirit to enter.
- If the person does NOT REPENT, then cut off ties with the person, telling them forgiveness and deliverance is available to them. If you do not cut off ties, they will worry you to death and destroy your peace.

The Jezebel needs to learn the meaning of the word "NO!"

So far, what has been explained is how to identify and possibly stop its activity. Understanding the roots of the Jezebel, and Healing for the person who has this spirit requires more insight.

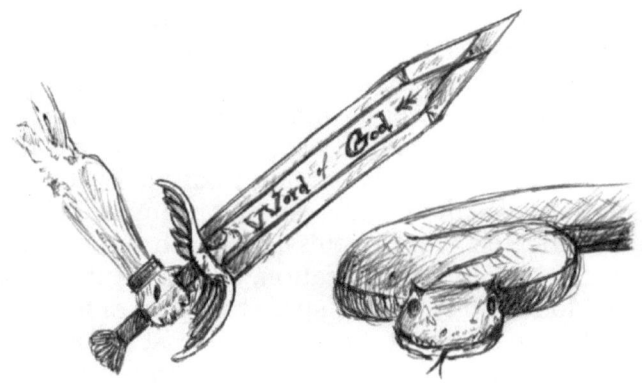

Chapter Thirteen
Jezebel and Divorce

Jezebel works hard to destroy relationships. This is especially true to cause divorce. Jezebel knows that a marriage is much stronger as one than and man or woman apart.

The Bible warns us about an evil spirit called jezebel and that we as Christians are not to tolerate this evil spirit.

Revelations 2:18-29 And unto the angel of the church in Thyatira write; These things saith the Son of God, who hath his eyes like unto a flame of fire, and his feet *are* like fine brass; I know thy works, and charity, and service, and faith, and thy patience, and thy works; and the last *to be* more than the first. Notwithstanding I have a few things against thee, because thou sufferest that woman Jezebel, which calleth herself a prophetess, to teach and to seduce my servants to commit fornication, and to eat things sacrificed unto idols. And I gave her space to repent of her fornication; and she repented not. Behold, I will cast her into a bed, and them that commit adultery with her into great tribulation, except they repent of their deeds. And I will kill her children with death; and all the churches shall know that I am he which searcheth the reins and hearts: and I will give unto every one of you according to your works. But unto you I say, and unto the rest in Thyatira, as many as have not this doctrine, and which have not known the depths of Satan, as they speak; I will put upon you none other burden. But that which ye have *already* hold fast till I come. And he that overcometh, and keepeth my works unto the end, to him will I give power over the nations: And he shall rule them with a rod of iron; as the vessels of a potter shall they be broken to shivers: even as I received of my Father. And I will give him the morning star. He that hath an ear, let him hear what the Spirit saith unto the churches.

The spirit of divorce has a name. The spirit of divorce is jezebel. Jezebel is the spirit of divorce.

Most of the books talk about "jezebel in the church", but as I watch the lives of friends and family, I can tell you that jezebel is in the home, our culture, our society, our churches and our government. Jesus has impressed upon me to write about this evil spirit called jezebel as I take my stand upon and under the authority of the Lord Jesus Christ of Nazareth.

The Bible in Genesis Chapter 3 credits satan as the one who attacked the very first husband and wife marriage on planet earth. Later, an Old Testament Queen called jezebel would provide the functional name of this evil spirit, which attacks every marriage in the United States and around the world. What I am trying to say to you is that the jezebel spirit existed long before it acquired its functional name from the Old Testament Queen called jezebel. In fact, we can see the operating style and method of the jezebel spirit way back in Genesis Chapter 3 as satan attacked and defeated Adam and Eve who had not yet inherited the fallen nature of sin.

Today, in the United States, at least 50% of all marriages end in divorce. The jezebel spirit is the spirit of divorce that destroys marriages. Just think, every person in the United States will be attacked by jezebel, and statistically, more than 50% of the nation have lost that battle – now that should get your attention!!

Although most authors explain that jezebel most often uses the woman as host and makes the man the target, Scripture gives example of jezebel using a man as the host to attack another man as the target. What the Holy Spirit has impressed upon me to explain is that the jezebel spirit attacks marriages (husbands and wives). The jezebel spirit is focused upon destroying the marriage relationship by targeting the husband, and gradually destroying the wife host. You must understand that if Adam and Eve where attacked back in the Garden of Eden, you have no chance of being overlooked by the devil. Again, jezebel attacks everyone and statistically more than 50% of the population end up losing that battle.

The operating style and method is revealed in Genesis:

- The planting of a lie... "Ye shall not surely die" Genesis 3:4
- The suggestion of mistrust... "For God doth know... your eyes shall be opened" Genesis 3:5

It's that simple – a false accusation (a lie) plus the suggestion that the target (in this case God the Father) should not be trusted. As you can see, the devil called God Almighty a "liar" by saying "Ye shall not surely die." Then the devil suggested mistrust by saying that God Almighty did not have Adam and Eve's best interests in mind.

> James 4:7 Submit yourselves therefore to God. Resist the devil, and he will flee from you.

Adam and Eve did not submit to God – the devil deceived Eve to take God's authority into her own hands and Adam allowed it to happen as he watched her do it "...and gave also unto her husband with her and he did eat." (Genesis 3:6)

As a result of this mistake (sin) on the part of both Adam and Eve, and for reasons best known to Father God, God Almighty sovereignly decreed that the husband would be the head (the authority) over the marriage just as Jesus is the head (the authority) over the entire Body Of Christ. Because the husband is the person God Almighty set as authority over the marriage, then the evil spirit of jezebel attacks marriages just like the marriage of Adam and Eve – entice the wife not to submit to the husband's headship authority just as Eve was enticed not to submit to God's headship authority in the Garden of Eden.

The jezebel game is designed to destroy relationships. Now, the evil jezebel spirit has been around for thousands of years working it's curse on each new generation.

Before you try to help the person with the jezebel spirit – remember, you are the next target:

- Jezebel must destroy those they are afraid of because they have a spirit of fear, others are a threat to their security or position, they are highly insecure but will not admit it, and anyone who may expose them is the enemy.
- They are controlling, manipulative and subtle. They take credit for the accomplishments of others and have others overlooked.
- Lying is necessary to protect themselves from mistakes they make (but blame others for). They lie, and they know they are lying.
- They are narcissistic (in love with themselves only) and have no concern for the feelings of their victim. In fact they tend to play the role of victim themselves to gain support and sympathy. They are committed to only one thing – getting what they want no matter what the cost is to others.
- They quietly record criticisms from others and then manufacture false accusations to be released in secret meetings behind their victim's back. Of course they do not see this as gossip but label it as "sharing a concern."
- Absolutely masterful in attacking and denying, as jezebel will have you discredited or removed. Again, absolutely masterful in winning compassion and support from others by appearing to be an innocent bystander while making you look like the abusive

attacker by manipulating you into lets say frustration or anger. Will often cycle between being the attacker and being a victim which is done purposefully to confuse you. Careful investigation must be made to distinguish the real victim from the fake (jezebel) one.
- They rationalize and defend, but never admit they were wrong. The devil and his demons are masterful at masking, hiding and camouflaging. Therefore, in the husband and wife relationship, the jezebel spirit will launch it's attack through the host during PMS (the PreMenstrual cycle). So yes, PMS affects the woman's hormone levels, associated body chemicals and therefore accomplishes mood swings (tension, irritability, crying spells, anxiety, depression), but... just as the military launches their attack at night, jezebel launches it's attack during PMS so no one suspects demonic activity by saying "it's just PMS" when the truth is that it is PMS and a whole lot more.
- They are usually women but can be men. The women tend to control their men with sex. They pick passive men so they can dominate them.
- Jezebel will make false allegations and call the police. The father will get dragged through the courts multiple times in a few years. Each case involves hundreds of pages of documents that he has to answer as a result of new evidence or complaints and will spend days in court at a huge cost to defend himself.
- Psychological counseling will not help because the individual will both deny what they are and deny they have the evil spirit of jezebel motivating and/or controlling them. Jezebel lacks the internal emotional mechanisms to have healthy relationships because they have been emotionally damaged in early

childhood and are therefore emotionally and relationally underdeveloped. Think of the jezebel person as a "two-year-old."
- Under the control of a demonic spirit, the mental and emotional health of the jezebel will continue to deteriorate. The jezebel (sociopathic) mother will allow a new partner to sexually abuse a child in an effort to purposefully inflict emotional damage to the child and turn the child into a manipulative mini-me. The courts do not recognize the sociopathic woman as incapable of functioning as a mother nor does the court see the demonic aspect of the jezebel. The jezebel uses the child as a tool to manipulate and control the father and extract finances from the father. The father is left to helplessly watch as precious children suffer at the hands of their mother.

The Bible tells us that our battle is not with flesh and blood. Our battle is with evil spirits and demons influencing and/or controlling the person that needs help. Our job is to pray and intercede so that God Almighty can help the person who needs the help. If the person needing the help is unwilling to receive help from Jesus, we can still pray the curse breaking prayers for them on their behalf (Intercession: pleading on behalf of another person, a prayer to God on behalf of another):

The person needing help (the jezebel host, the jezebel target, the jezebel victims) will need to do the following simple formula to start receiving what they need from Jesus:

- Forgive and bless (say the words out loud, I choose to forgive others for what they did, I choose to not blame

you Jesus for what happened, I ask you Jesus to bless them, and I choose to forgive myself – all of that should be said out loud)
- Confess and repent (say the words out loud, I confess that I did not handle the situation perfectly, I choose to repent by looking to God for help rather than what I was doing)
- Ask Jesus to forgive you, cleanse you, and heal you (again say those words out loud, I ask you Jesus to forgive, cleanse and heal me).

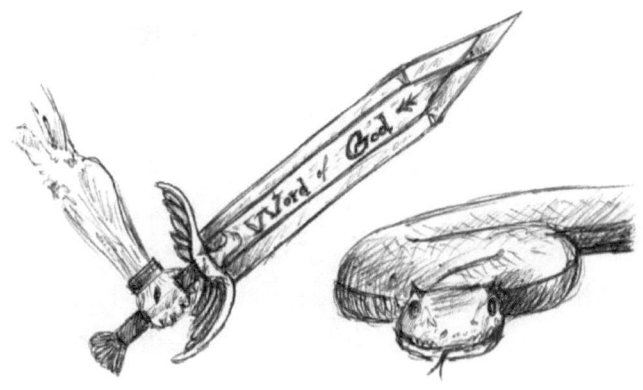

Chapter Fourteen

The Jezebel Culture

The Jezebel Spirit has a way of taking their world and adding it to the Church. The Jezebel principality always desires to assert its own will in the world. You can find this principality's handiwork in nearly every organized political system, behind the lust for power. Working behind the scenes through deception and manipulation, Jezebel weakens the authority of sincere leaders to govern effectively.

In America cultures today, Jezebel is the driving force behind a large number of issues and movements that set people and their values against the will of God. Those with liberal mindsets mock spiritual values and moral standards such as the sanctity of marriage and reserving sex for the confines of marriage, while at the same time condoning homosexuality—for starters. Jezebel is hugely influential in the areas of extreme male dominance, the lack of freedom or rights for women and dictators who rule with ruthless control.

The abortion controversy in the United States is just one example of how the Jezebel principality grossly affects our culture. Our culture has made a baby in the womb nothing more than cellular tissue. People are urged to believe that abortion is acceptable. The Church as a whole has stood against such killings. But in the same manner in which Queen Jezebel came against the prophetic leadership of Elijah, the Jezebel principality continues to come against the anointing of the Church. It makes every attempt to destroy the Church's credibility and relevance in the world. It seeks to minimize people's belief and confidence in a Holy God by attacking the very nature of God, which is life. Its influence on abortion is a strategic position of power for Jezebel. Jezebel is also behind the satanic lie that has been fed to our youth—"Do whatever feels good, and don't worry about the consequences."

Not only has the issue of abortion brought destruction to millions of lives, it has also divided a people who have been made righteous by the cross against themselves. Even church denominations now passionately disagree on the issue of taking innocent life. And as the Church, we are the ultimate prize the kingdom of darkness focuses on for destruction.

> John 10:10 The thief cometh not, but for to steal, and to kill, and to destroy: I am come that they might have life, and that they might have it more abundantly.

The women's rights movement is another example of how the Jezebel principality uses an issue to terribly influence culture. The agenda of this movement in the United States has never been just about freedom for women. This is not to say that good has not come from the movement. Women now enjoy unparalleled parity with men and freedom like no other time in history, especially in Western cultures. They increasingly have the right to choose and to express themselves as free moral agents, within the protection of society. Less restricted and unhindered in personal and professional aspirations, they now can follow the blueprint God has placed within them. They enjoy better jobs and freedom to be in the workplace, and their contribution in education is more recognized. Tragically, however, just like many men, many women have not looked to the Word of God and to God Himself to find their identity.

In understanding the history of the women's movement, though, you would by and large find that its motivation is more about dominance—not just gaining women's freedom, even from the dominance of men, but asserting women's "right" to dominate others. Women's rights is therefore not truly an equality issue in every situation; it is also about control through supremacy. Jezebel by its nature seeks to tower above anyone or anything else. Interestingly, this is the same characteristic Lucifer displayed in his rebellion against God. Isaiah 14:13–14 tells us what Lucifer said in his heart:

> Isaiah 14:13, 14 For thou hast said in thine heart, I will ascend into heaven, I will exalt my throne above the stars of God: I will sit also upon the mount of the congregation, in the sides of the north: I will ascend above the heights of the clouds; I will be like the most High.

Lucifer is a defeated foe, yet in league with the Jezebel principality and others of his evil realm, he gains power by changing the focus of people away from a righteous God. The kingdom of darkness only has to influence the thinking of a few through lies and half-truths to gain a stronghold in the minds and imaginations of the whole.

Today's popular movies and modern music are filled with violence, filthiness, sexual uncleanliness and disrespect for authority and for the personhood of others. Nothing is left to the imagination; sexual images are graphically depicted in an effort to make sure we get the point. Like Satan, whom Genesis 3:1 described as "cunning" in his encounter with Eve in the Garden, the Jezebel principality is insidious and crafty in its use of these images. It directs, influences and gains control over people's minds through the use of images now enhanced through technology. Technological advances provide the multitudes with easy access to a flood of perverted images that overflow their rebellious and carnal minds, which have become the devil's strongholds.

Think about the sitcoms that undermine the family and male authority, which are largely written by homosexuals (with an Ahab spirit) who have found acceptance from those with a far-left agenda. Talk shows, which more and more exalt unrighteous thinking, are also ruled by Jezebel. So is much of the fashion industry. Then there's the pornography industry, perhaps Jezebel's most effective arena. Jezebel runs unchallenged through our avenues of entertainment. This principality is preeminent throughout Hollywood, which seems the most subservient of all to its agenda.

These words in the book of Revelation are apropos to the battle in this present day:

> Revelations 12:15 And the serpent cast out of his mouth water as a flood after the woman, that he might cause her to be carried away of the flood.

There is no question that this flood out of the serpent's mouth is the sinister deceitfulness and warring of the devil, as his destructive thrust "flows" through the electronic airwaves. This flood of words and forbidden images is now so commonplace and overwhelming that we live in acceptance of it. The prophet Jeremiah could have been describing our society when he said, "No! They were not at all ashamed; nor did they know how to blush" (Jeremiah 6:15; 8:12). We have become desensitized. We are no longer shocked and embarrassed by obscene talk or behavior.

The rebellious Jezebel principality is the spirit of witchcraft (1 Samuel 15:23). As understood from a biblical perspective, witchcraft is anything that usurps the authority and influence of the Holy Spirit in a person's life. The World English Dictionary defines witchcraft as "the art, power or act of bringing magical or paranormal power to bear through fascination, bewitching influence or charm." From this understanding, we can surmise that the imagery used by Hollywood and other sources precludes, or at best attempts to invalidate, the picture that the Holy Spirit desires to paint in the hearts and minds of people.

Contrary to this manipulation of others' minds, the apostle Paul repeatedly stated that he was commending himself and the Gospel to the consciences of men, not trying to manipulate, but to convince them. Like it or not, all of mankind is involved in the middle of a war. Both the Kingdom of God and the kingdom of darkness are engaged in a battle for our minds. In Ephesians, Paul described how wrong thinking and unholy living have the potential to separate a person from the blessings of God that flow through clean living and righteous thinking:

> Ephesians 5:3-7 But fornication, and all uncleanness, or covetousness, let it not be once named among you, as becometh saints; Neither filthiness, nor foolish talking, nor jesting, which are not convenient: but rather giving of thanks. For this ye know, that no whoremonger, nor unclean person, nor covetous man, who is an idolater, hath any inheritance in the kingdom of Christ and of God. Let no man deceive you with vain words: for because of these things cometh the wrath of God upon the children of disobedience. Be not ye therefore partakers with them.

When people engage in these things contrary to God, they miss out on the abundant life here and now. Contrary to the popular statement by the Hollywood culture that says, "We are simply imitating society in what we produce," in reality people are mimicking onscreen the depravity of their own hearts. Following their darkened hearts and vain imaginations, they give themselves over to all manner of evil, as Paul described in Romans 1:21:

> Romans 1:21 Because that, when they knew God, they glorified him not as God, neither were thankful; but became vain in their imaginations, and their foolish heart was darkened.

These people indeed have a knowledge of God, but because they do not glorify or acknowledge Him and because they are unthankful, they are doomed to futile thoughts and darkened hearts. Read the rest of Romans chapter 1, which further shows the slippery slope into depravity that people who live this way are on.

The twisted use of the Internet has made available to the masses inconceivably destructive images and thoughts, which have entered the minds of males and females alike. Several countries have banned the spread of pornography and other destructive materials in an effort to limit the effect on their culture. But like its mentor, Satan, the Jezebel principality ultimately desires to replace righteous thinking with unholy images and thoughts, thereby turning individuals away from the life they could find in God.

Jezebel is not only visible in society; this principality comes to church! In Revelation 2:20, the apostle John talked about a spiritual woman, a so-called "prophetess," who was an idol worshiper: "Nevertheless I have a few things against you, because you allow that woman Jezebel, who calls herself a prophetess, to teach and seduce My servants to commit sexual immorality and eat things sacrificed to idols." In the early

Church, as Gentiles became part of the Kingdom, they brought with them customs, philosophies and patterns of living that were not always in accordance with the godly precepts found in the Old Testament. One of these issues was their accustomed form of worship. They worshiped idols with animal sacrifices, which was similar to Jewish worship. But when Gentiles worshiped, their main departure was that they also included sex as part of their rituals. The sex was "between consenting adults"—male or female—with multiple partners if desired.

In Acts 15:19–20, the apostles addressing this issue at the Jerusalem council. After the council reached an agreement, Peter issued this edict in the form of a hand-delivered letter pronouncing their judgment:

> Acts 15:19, 20 Wherefore my sentence is, that we trouble not them, which from among the Gentiles are turned to God: But that we write unto them, that they abstain from pollutions of idols, and from fornication, and from things strangled, and from blood.

The concern was that idol worship was tied to rebellion, iniquity (sin) and witchcraft. When these are present, the Word of the Lord is rejected. It is amazing how closely this correlates with what the prophet Samuel said in his rebuke of Saul in the Old Testament:

> 1 Samuel 15:23 For rebellion is as the sin of witchcraft, and stubbornness is as iniquity and idolatry. Because thou hast rejected the word of the LORD, he hath also rejected thee from being king.

In a word, beware of those who believe it is their place to "help you" hear from God about your call or ministry. They probably have a self-serving agenda. The anointing is what helps you:

> 1 John 2:27 But the anointing which ye have received of him abideth in you, and ye need not that any man teach you: but as the same anointing teacheth you of all things, and is truth, and is no lie, and even as it hath taught you, ye shall abide in him.

Jezebel deceives with the right words and wrong spirit. A Jezebel spirit overcomes people through the weakness of their flesh, appealing to them through their fear, insecurity, wrong concepts of authority and the like. Jezebel will use any effective means, but some of its favorites are lust, sex, gossip, manipulation and false accusations.

In several instances in the book of Acts, the apostles going into new places met Jezebel deceivers. They dealt with them either through the gift of the discerning of spirits or by exercising their authority as believers. Peter had to confront Simon, the sorcerer in Samaria who wanted to buy the power he saw the apostles display when they laid hands on someone and the person received the Holy Spirit. Peter rebuked Simon for his evil motive and unrepentant heart (Acts 8:9–24). Paul rebuked an evil spirit of divination on a slave girl at Philippi who kept disrupting the ministry by following Paul and crying out that he and his companions were servants of God. Angering her masters by freeing her from the spirit, Paul and Silas were beaten and thrown into prison (Acts 16:16–24).

As is evident from these examples, the idolatry of Jezebel involves a love for power and authority. A skilled Jezebel can sense authority and wants to weaken it or take it away, as did those whom Peter and Paul met. Jezebel's idolatry is so strong that those with a controlling spirit will literally destroy others' lives, with no remorse, to gain what they seek. Just like Queen Jezebel in the Old Testament, Jezebel today is quick to shed blood and lead others into deeper idolatry than ever before.

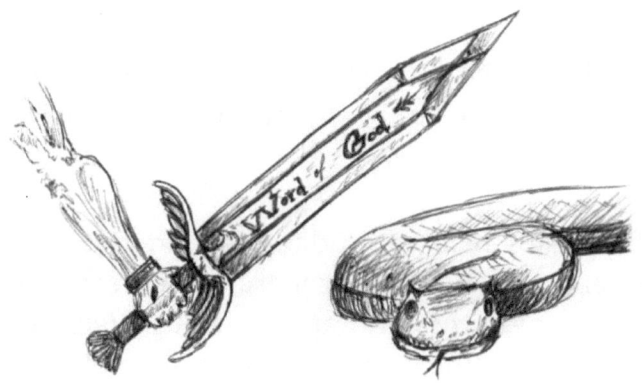

Chapter Fifteen
Wounds and Jezebel

You may not realize it in the heat of the fight against this spirit, but there are wounds that the devils plants this spirit into. Confronting this spirit is not as easy as it may seem. It is hard to diagnose, due to its many faces. One minute, it can appear prayerfully submissive and the next it can act bold and brash. Or it may simply appear to be concerned for the wellbeing of the church. Like an octopus with eight spindly arms, this spirit is a nightmare to dislodge. Before confronting someone with a Jezebel spirit, a pastor must first assess his or her own personal and spiritual condition. Danger lies in being tempted to react defensively and to misuse your power.

If a pastor feels intimidated by previous encounters with a Jezebel spirit, future scenarios may leave him or her feeling bitter, resentful, and angry. If these feelings exist, it simply signals that the pastor is not ready to effectively deal with this spirit. Before going further, the pastor may need to appoint someone with wisdom, discernment, and spiritual authority, as well as a "eunuch mentality" to help. This may require that a pastor look for a specialist in deliverance ministry.

Those who are going to address the Jezebel spirit operating through a person must first pause and assess their own spiritual condition. Ask yourself: Are you feeling any jealousy, strife, envy, or malice toward a past or present authority figure in your life? Do you harbor any hidden feelings of rejection or being overlooked?

Such feelings may lead you to overreact to the Jezebel spirit. Until these attitudes are overcome, addressing a spirit of insubordination and rebellion in another cannot be fully or powerfully accomplished. In addition, there are other issues to be dealt with.

> Galatians 6:1 Brethren, if a man be overtaken in a fault, ye which are spiritual, restore such an one in the spirit of meekness; considering thyself, lest thou also be tempted.

If a pastor has not dealt immediately with each issue that has arisen, they must deal with their frustration and anger that may have mounted. No one likes to be controlled by another person. If a pastor has been wounded by someone with a Jezebel spirit, then he or she is an ideal candidate for mishandling a ministry situation. Scripture warns us:

> James 1:20 For the wrath of man worketh not the righteousness of God.

Since an individual with a Jezebel spirit often uses criticism and accusation, such demonic spirits cannot be driven out by a pastor who reacts in like manner. A pastor must first confront and deal with his or her own critical and accusing spirit.

When control and manipulation are evidenced in a pastor's life, he or she will become defenseless against a Jezebel spirit. In counteracting manipulation with manipulation, the pastor will have failed to walk in the fruit of the Holy Spirit. Moreover, God does not honor our actions when we return evil for evil.

Whenever we react this way, our anger has twice the impact. First, we lash out because we are angry with ourselves for allowing the wound to remain in our soul. Second, we react because we are angry with the person who manifests the same tendency toward sin. We are often guilty of attacking the very weaknesses in others that are evidence in our lives.

When pastors feel insecure or uncertain of how to handle a situation, they may resort to intimidation. They do this to maintain control. Intimidation, however, will never bring true repentance or restoration, which should always be our goal. Intimidation will only produce a temporary remorse, feigned repentance, or withdrawal. Intimidation will abort any sincere opportunity to minister healing to a wounded person.

Attempting to create fear in someone else by appearing more powerful will only complicate the problem. It will drive a pastor to badger, belittle, and attempt to "back the person into a corner." Such methods will only birth more hostility. Or it will provoke the individual to stir up slander or plan acts of violence and rage.

When a pastor reacts to a Jezebelite in anger, the Jezebelite will begin to appear to tremble. Such individuals will portray themselves as being a victim and you as being an monster. This usually happens whenever others are present to witness your angry outburst, which will make it seem as if the Jezebelite is the underdog. If you haven't already experienced this, you will. It is only a matter of time.

Instinctively, individuals with a Jezebel spirit will often mirror a pastor's manner of operation. If the pastor is self-promoting, such individuals may feel the freedom to promote their own gifts and abilities. If the leader is domineering, individuals may see this as granting permission to maintain the upper hand at all times with others. If a domineering pastor clashes with such strong-willed Jezebels, a fierce and ugly battle will arise.

I recommend that a pastor focus his or her attention on opposing the demonic stronghold in the person while demonstrating love toward the person. Any confrontation must be done in love in order to restore the Jezebelite. Only a loving confrontation will induce an individual to experience brokenness. He or she will need to experience godly sorrow that leads to repentance.

If you face resistance by the Jezebelite, avoid the tendency to react scornfully. Remember, you are not wrestling against flesh and blood, but against the powers of darkness (Ephesians 6:12). Ask God to search your heart further. Then respond with great strength and determination to help the individual repent. If you are defensive or reactive, the Jezebelite may detect your insecurity and respond with a mask of meekness meant to disarm you. Your confidence must be in the Lord. Believing that God has appointed you as shepherd over the flock will enable you to act valiantly and with compassion.

Memories of neglect from a mother, from prior romantic relationships, or from fluctuations in a marriage influence a pastor's ability to communicate and confront. Jezebelites will usually sense a pastor's bitterness or areas of unresolved wounds. Therefore, a pastor must guard against transferring unconscious and unsettled issues about a grandmother, mother, sister, or spouse to individuals operating under a Jezebel spirit.

Suspicion, strife, and vain imagination about potential conflicts will tempt a pastor to eliminate anyone who seems unsubmissive. However suspicion, strife, and vain imagination are spirits of witchcraft. If a pastor is tempted to operate in these ways, such spirits may obtain a foothold in him or her. A pastor will not be able to overcome a Jezebel spirit until freed of these heart issues. Furthermore, demonic spirits may attack a pastor or leader who arrogantly or smugly attacks a Jezebel spirit.

To operate in the wrong spirit is sometimes described as operating in the power of the soul. Whenever we use our soul to conquer another's soul, we fail to get God's needed counsel to gain victory. Only by exercising the fruits of the Holy Spirit— love, joy, peace, longsuffering, kindness, goodness, faithfulness, gentleness, and self-control—can the power of the soul be conquered. Remember, a spiritual touch can produce eternal change in another. Trying to use the soul in this manner will bring disaster to a pastor, his or her family, and the church.

A pastor must keep in mind that he or she is dealing with dark powers. This battle is not merely with a person. The enemy's success distorts our thinking and produces a spirit of fear, suspicion, or accusation in our hearts. The Jezebel spirit operates under the power of the soul. If you operate under the same power, you inflate the demonic spirit and it now controls both of you.

You will need to encourage a person who has repented from using a Jezebel spirit to continue taking new steps forward. He or she must be encouraged to keep renewing his or her mind, learning to recognize and adopt God's way of looking at things.

Activities that restore feelings of self-worth should be encouraged. Frequently, these individuals have a great desire to contribute in a worthwhile way. Servanthood, with healthy boundaries, is a key to restoration. However, their serving others should not be confused with their having authority. To give them authority at this time would be equal to giving an alcoholic a drink.

All areas of rebellion will need to be addressed. In an attitude of meekness, amends will need to be made in order to close the door to future inroads by the enemy.

For pastors who must confront an individual who operates with a Jezebel spirit, here are my suggestions:

- Seek counsel about any personal blind spots or weaknesses you have from those who are spiritually mature.
- Pray before you speak in any confrontation. Ask the Holy Spirit to reveal hidden issues. If you allow the Holy Spirit to do His work, it is amazing how issues will surface that had not been previously known.
- Ask the Holy Spirit for wisdom to discern what is spiritual, by discerning what demonic spirits the individual has embraced. Ask for discernment about what is natural or from the person's upbringing, such as harsh parental issues.
- Avoid becoming angry at all costs! Keep calm. Do not overreact or make the issue larger than it is.
- Do not ignore the problem! It will not disappear.
- From the moment a problem is suspected, document all third-party information. Record dates, times, places, and what was said. Otherwise, trying to piece together tidbits of information will only lead to the person's denial.
- During a confrontation, always have someone in the room with you.
- Confront each issue with grace, but with firmness and candor. Be specific. You must explain the problems. However do not make the mistake of revealing names and specific accusations.
- Get permission from third parties to use all testimonies, along with their names, in the meeting. If

you do not, the Jezebelite will deny ever having said such things.
- Tape record the meeting. Be sure to let the individual know that you are taping the meeting. Set the tape recorder in the open for all to see.

If you follow these suggestions, be prepared for Jezebel to repent and apologize with great passion. However, do not be surprised when Jezebel, whom you thought had repented, recoils and strikes again with greater vengeance. If that happens, simply repeat the above process of confrontation. If the person will not hear you the second time, then you must remove him or her from the church.

Here are some early warning signs that pastors, in hindsight, have shared with me. Pastors may want to keep alert for these phrases that could indicate a storm is brewing on the horizon.

- "I just want to be your friend." More than likely, people who say these things will have expectations that you will never be able to meet.
- "I just want to help you get to where God has called you." In other words, "you cannot get to your destiny without me." Beware!
- "There are no strings attached to my help. I just want to serve." However, you'll find lots of hidden strings.
- "You can trust me. I will always support you." Such people will support you as long as you do what they say!
- "You do not acknowledge my gifting." People like this are asking you for more authority in the church.

- "You do not understand me." This is a veiled cry for you to spend more time with them than you have available.
- "You intimidate me. I do not feel like I can talk to you." In other words, "My goals should become your goals."
- "I have new revelation. The pastor has Old Testament understanding and I have New Testament understanding." In other words, "I am right and you are wrong!"
- "The Lord has given me some things that I need to share with you." Duck! You'll probably be receiving a harsh spanking.
- "My last pastor did not know how to use me or my gifts." In other words, they are saying, "Let me have my way."

If handled rightly, an attack by a Jezebel spirit will ultimately strengthen a church. God uses the fiery battles of life to train, strengthen, and refine us (1 Peter 4:12-19). As God once told me: Small battles produce small victories, but great battles produce great victories—in our lives, in our ministries, and in our churches.

Chapter Sixteen

The Power of the Jehu Mantle

There is one person in the Word of God that overcame Jezebel. This Mantle is available for us to operate in the authority of Jehu. There is much to learn from Jehu. God anointed him to end Jezebel's horrific reign (by her death), to destroy the house of Ahab (by taking the lives of his seventy sons) and to kill the worshipers of Baal with the sword (2 Kings 9:30-10:28). The mantle of authority with which Jehu carried out his mission is revealed within his name and his generational lineage.

Iniquity, attaches itself as a bondage and afflicts families down to the third and fourth generations. But there is also a positive side to this movement down generational lines: Godly family destinies and mantles of authority can also be passed from one generation to another, and these can destroy yokes! Jehu was a third generation of many who were named after powerful attributes of Jehovah. This shows why we need to become free from all bondage—in order to empower the next generation to do the same.

First, Jehu's grandfather (I am considering him the "first generation" that had an anointing) was named Nimshi. (2 Kings 9:2.) His name translates as "one who sets free" and "rescued." We can conclude, therefore, considering the importance of names in that culture, that God had removed a yoke of some type from Nimshi. This needed to be accomplished so that a mantle of authority could be passed to the next generation. This mantle represented the anointing to break yokes and set people free, obviously rescuing them from destroying yokes of oppression Thus, we notice the mandate of Isaiah 10:27 once again:

> Isaiah 10:27 And it shall come to pass in that day, that his burden shall be taken away from off thy shoulder, and his yoke from off thy neck, and the yoke shall be destroyed because of the anointing.

God desires that certain events come to pass, especially for bondages to be destroyed by an anointing. God will always use mankind in His plans upon the earth. I believe the generations of Jehu were destined to be carriers of God's anointing and that this anointing was used to destroy God's enemies. The anointing to set people free was on its way to Jehu. I shudder to think what might have happened if the mantle had never been passed to him!

The name of Jehu's father, Jehoshaphat, when translated means "Jehovah judges." When considering the anointing required to set people free, I can also imagine just how someone might need to be reminded that it is always God who is doing the judging. I believe that this might be where the Christian cliché "We hate the evil, but we love the person manifesting the evil" originated. It is not our responsibility to judge; we are called only to discern the evil spirits and cast them out in order to remove the bondages.

Jehovah God is the righteous Judge; we are simply the obedient vessels He uses in the process to carry out His directives. God will always work His plans through the hearts of His people—but it is His power at work, and we can never forget that. As believers we can discern the presence of an evil spirit—or that a person is allowing the evil spirit to operate through him or her—but any judging must always be left up to God.

When we examine Isaiah 10:27, we see that it was God who was destroying the yokes. Notice that He refers to Himself as "the Lord of Hosts," who accomplishes this:

> Isaiah 10:24-27 Therefore thus saith the Lord GOD of hosts, O my people that dwellest in Zion, be not afraid of the

> Assyrian: he shall smite thee with a rod, and shall lift up his staff against thee, after the manner of Egypt. For yet a very little while, and the indignation shall cease, and mine anger in their destruction. And the LORD of hosts shall stir up a scourge for him according to the slaughter of Midian at the rock of Oreb: and as his rod was upon the sea, so shall he lift it up after the manner of Egypt. And it shall come to pass in that day, that his burden shall be taken away from off thy shoulder, and his yoke from off thy neck, and the yoke shall be destroyed because of the anointing.

It is God's own power that breaks yokes. There is no reason for any of us to become puffed up when He uses us powerfully. We might be anointed, but that is only because He is anointed.

Jehu's name translates as "Jehovah is." Now this is where your imagination can really become active.

> Micah 2:13 The breaker is come up before them: they have broken up, and have passed through the gate, and are gone out by it: and their king shall pass before them, and the LORD on the head of them.

Jesus desires to "break through" for us and at the same time "break bondages"—truly He is the "Breaker." Yes, Christ, the Breaker, desires to break us out of the old patterns that have contained us and at the same time break us into our future! Whatever has seemed barren and desolate in your life due to the bondages upon you is now becoming alive. It is not up to us to make this happen—our complete dependence must be on Him. This is why "Jehovah is!"

Someone anointed by God to defeat Jezebel must be someone in close relationship with God—intimate and in covenant with Him which would mean that "Jehovah God is everything." We live for Him and all that we do is committed to Him. He is our strength and our salvation. Then, as we obey, it is completely up to Him to judge our enemies. We, as co-laborers in Christ, given power and authority over the enemy (especially Jezebel), are not the ones in power. When Elisha's servant anointed Jehu to defeat Baal worshipers and Jezebel, queen of Israel, it was never "Jehu's power" that defeated God's enemies. Jehu responded to that call with God's own power and zeal.

When Jehu was anointed, he was addressed as captain (2 Kings 9:5, 11), which means "commander." Jehu had a commanding anointing—and so do we!

One of the words used in the Old Testament for command is tsavah. This Hebrew word implies putting things in order through commanding. It also refers to someone who is appointed and charged to fulfill a responsibility. Jehu was "charged" and "appointed" by God to fulfill his destiny.

Jehu had mighty victories under that anointing and mantle, but he defeated the false god Baal to a large degree before he ever went into battle. He waited until his time, even though he was fully possessed with great zeal. God had told Elijah that Jehu would be crowned king of Israel and would bring God's vengeance on the worshipers of Baal. Yet it was not until Elisha succeeded Elijah that Jehu was released to his mission. If you recall, Baal, the god of Jezebel, promotes fornication—desiring something, especially religious promotion or power, before God's timing.

I referred earlier to Jeremiah who also was appointed by God to perform a specific task. He was given a charge by God to fulfill a certain responsibility. When Jeremiah was able to see his future, he was then empowered with zeal to fulfill it. This is why it is so very important for us to see all that God has for us, which includes our future, our calling, our anointing and destiny. When Jeremiah said, "I see the branch of an almond tree budding," he was seeing his future. How is that? Well, the almond tree is the first tree that blooms in a new season. Jeremiah saw his new season. Oppressions of fear were broken off of him as he "saw." God said to him that he was seeing correctly, and then He said this:

> Jeremiah 1:11, 12 Moreover the word of the LORD came unto me, saying, Jeremiah, what seest thou? And I said, I see a rod of an almond tree. Then said the LORD unto me, Thou hast well seen: for I will hasten my word to perform it.

When we see it, we can have it! And the benefits applied are this: God will "watch" over His promise and then "fulfill" it. When God watches over His words, this means that He promises to remain alert and on the lookout for us—watching over us to ensure that we fulfill our potential. Wow! What a promise to hold on to! And please take a moment to ponder this also: God gives us the ability to take command in our own lives. This is all the result of a supernatural zeal that comes when we step into our God-given authority—or when we "see" our future and are willing to walk in God's perfect timing. This is another way we can break off bondages of oppression: We "see" them broken.

Yet, all the while, we must realize that our mantles of zeal come from the Lord Himself Read the inspiring passage below and notice that Jesus took it upon Himself to deliver us from every evil bondage. When He looked upon us and saw that there was no justice, He desired to intervene on our behalf He put on His own righteousness and garments of vengeance (against our enemy!) and then clothed Himself with zeal. This was all done on our behalf

> Isaiah 59:15-17 Yea, truth faileth; and he that departeth from evil maketh himself a prey: and the LORD saw it, and it displeased him that there was no judgment. And he saw that there was no man, and wondered that there was no intercessor: therefore his arm brought salvation unto him; and his righteousness, it sustained him. For he put on righteousness as a breastplate, and an helmet of salvation upon his head; and he put on the garments of vengeance for clothing, and was clad with zeal as a cloke.

In Acts we are urged to Remember that Jezebel is a false prophetess operating in divination and the occult. It is clear that Paul had a "commanding anointing":

Paul became so troubled that he turned around and said to the spirit, in the name of Jesus Christ I command you to come out of her!" At that moment the spirit left her.

Who cannot testify that the apostle Paul had a mantle to destroy yokes of Jezebel and deception just as Jehu did? Though he did not have this slave girl thrown out of a window to her death, as Jehu commanded concerning Jezebel, nonetheless he destroyed the yoke of Jezebel upon her life.

For one to be a commander requires not only courage but also strength—full strength! Jehu's zeal empowered him to move full force against God's enemies. More on that in a minute. Jehu was anointed by God and instructed to smite the house of Ahab so that God could,

> 2 Kings 9:7 And thou shalt smite the house of Ahab thy master, that I may avenge the blood of my servants the prophets, and the blood of all the servants of the LORD, at the hand of Jezebel.

The word smite is the Hebrew word nakah. It means to strike, beat, wound, kill and clap in the sense of placing the enemy between your hands and, as you clap over your victory, crushing the devil.

> 2 Kings 9:24 And Jehu drew a bow with his full strength, and smote Jehoram between his arms, and the arrow went out at his heart, and he sunk down in his chariot.

Full strength means just what it says—every ounce of energy and determination that Jehu had went into drawing back his bow to defeat his enemy. This is exactly what is required as we defeat every bondage of Jezebel. We cannot be half-committed to this—that would actually be tolerating Jezebel, and Jesus rebuked the church of Thyatira for that very reason.

Where does godly zeal originate? From God, of course! Let's observe Scripture concerning this. It involves governmental authority, which actually originates in heaven:

Isaiah 9:6, 7 For unto us a child is born, unto us a son is given: and the government shall be upon his shoulder: and his name shall be called Wonderful, Counsellor, The mighty God, The everlasting Father, The Prince of Peace. Of the increase of his government and peace there shall be no end, upon the throne of David, and upon his kingdom, to order it, and to establish it with judgment and with justice from henceforth even for ever. The zeal of the LORD of hosts will perform this.

Keep this in mind: When Jezebel is in operation, there is no peace. Jesus is the Prince of Peace, and He has the eternal zeal to establish the increase of His government on this earth. He desired to use Jehu—and He did—to establish a level of governmental authority over Jezebel and Baal. He wants to use us also; will we submit to co-laboring with Him? I pray that you answer yes in your heart.

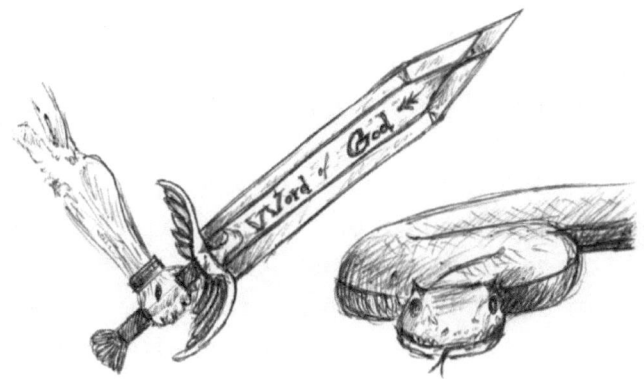

Chapter Seventeen

False Prophecy and Jezebel

When someone has the Jezebel Spirit they seem very prophetic. The big problem most Christians don't realize that they're as much a false prophet as they are Jezebel. It goes hand and hand. The Jezebel spirit is a deceitful impostor within the Church. It counterfeits the true prophetic gift, and it imitates and criticizes the proper function of prophetic ministries. Other darker counterfeits to the prophetic—psychics, clairvoyants, palm-readers who practice witchcraft, divination, and sorcery—have arisen to speak about the supernatural. However, a Jezebel spirit is more deceptive, simply because it is less obvious to the untrained eye, and it parades on scriptural grounds.

Although an individual given over to a Jezebel spirit may not practice the black arts or the deep secrets of Satan, they share the same clandestine, demonic roots with those in the occult. In fact, individuals controlled by a Jezebel spirit often bear greater fruit, because their actions are more covert and their roots become more entrenched before becoming detected.

Every church that embraces a prophetic ministry will have to contend with the Jezebel spirit because this demonic spirit mimics the prophetic gifts and callings of God. This spirit actually comes to destroy the prophetic gift. Consequently, it works covertly and its activities are extremely treacherous. Individuals given over to this spirit often try to enhance and strengthen their powerbase by attracting and controlling others, acting much like a spiritual magnet. Pastors and leaders will need to recognize the working of this covert spirit because it will seek to divide groups and stir up contention, confusion, and deception in the Church.

A clear distinction must be made between an immature prophetic person and someone who has a Jezebel spirit. Those who are prophetically immature are merely trying to find their rightful place in the Body. They may lack wisdom and humility, however their intention is not to destroy the church. Over eager and immature prophetic individuals will do things that seem foolish or unwise. But just as we don't kill our children for their immaturity, neither should we kill those who are in prophetic infancy. Pastors and leaders must make allowances for a young prophetic individual's childishness. Pastors and leaders must overcome their weariness of having young prophets who need to be trained.

As we—in the wisdom and counsel of the Lord—sharpen and hone the skills of those with prophetic gifts, it will bring forth valor and purity in the prophetic ministry. Eventually, such individuals will bring insight, revelation, and wisdom to the Body of Christ. Thus, all the petty difficulties of this development period will seem worth the time and effort expended.

During this developmental season, it's especially important not to maim or abort the gifts of young prophetic Christians by accusing them of having a Jezebel spirit. Pastors and leaders must learn to discern how to bring correction and how to nurture budding prophetic gifts, without wounding or killing people's spirits.

Sometimes the difference between an immature prophetic person and someone who operates with an immature Jezebel spirit is very subtle. To discern the difference involves looking at the heart of the matter. A young prophetic person begins with a heart to serve God. Those operating with a Jezebel spirit may have started out with a heart to serve God, but at some point they have departed from that path into one of self-promotion. Several additional points of departure are described more fully below.

Selfish Ambition

As Scripture advises us:

> Philippians 2:3 Let nothing be done through strife or vainglory; but in lowliness of mind let each esteem other better than themselves.

Individuals with a Jezebel spirit, loving the praise of others, will often give themselves a title or seek after a leadership position. Demonstrating superiority, they will regard a certain position as being "the most anointed" and dismiss another as being "less anointed" or as not having a voice in the church or in spiritual matters.

They will become zealous to market their gifts and broaden their sphere of influence. Often such individuals will not consult the Lord about where and when to minister. They will simply yield to the need for greater press. As their success increases, they will run to deliver many words, although God has not sent them. They may even believe that as their reputation increases, God's Kingdom will also increase. However, they are sadly deceived.

On the other hand, young prophetic individuals may gravitate initially toward the distinction push on them. But as they mature, most will shun any fanfare or publicity. They will realize that being in the limelight only serves to blind their eyes to God's high calling and that fame actually detracts from spending time alone with the Lord.

Individuals who are called to prophetic ministry must also desire to be held accountable for their words and actions. They should welcome others pointing out their errors and weaknesses. They must learn to submit to spiritual authority.

One of the trademarks of those with the heart of God is how they respond to correction. Those with a Jezebel spirit chafe when corrected, but those operating under the Holy Spirit will repent.

In the process of submission, they learn to die to self-will. This is an incredibly painful process, but all of us must pay the price and crucify our soul, as well as our fleshly desires. Willingness to submit every aspect of life and ministry to the Lord must be evident in those who stand to lead His Church.

Personal Gain

While a prophetic person goes through a costly breaking process (Nehemiah 5:14-19), an individual with a Jezebelite rarely makes such sacrifices. For the most part, a Jezebelite will express a persistent drive to demonstrate his or her "prophetic insight." In doing so, he or she has an ulterior motive and will insist upon some sort of payback—recognition, fame, money, clothing, or various privileges lavished upon him or her by individuals easily infatuated with supernatural insight.

Quickly, this self-centered individual will notice their prophetic insight can open doors. Consequently, he or she will give into the temptation to use their gift, mixed with human prognostication and personal opinion. Such an individual may read people's souls and later present their soulish insight as divinely inspired prophecy. When this tainted revelation comes forth, it will lead astray those who are not in tune with the Holy Spirit. So while the Jezebel spirit seeks to tear apart, the prophetic ministry seeks to serve and to encourage others and leave the hearer with a sense of hope.

A Lust for Life

Sensual appetites will often run rampant in individuals who operate with a Jezebel spirit. A spirit of lust will eat away at their soul, until it gains control of them. Such lust is not simply sexually oriented. Money, favor, or recognition may feed their ambition and offer desired results. An insatiable thirst for self-indulgent pleasures will grow. Conversely, the work of the Cross will cease to be manifested in this person's life.

Demonic Entanglement

As individuals approach an intermediate level of demonic entanglement, their purposes will become more cunning and deliberate. These individuals will try to control the actions of friends, families, and churches. Whenever false humility, lies, and flattery do not bring about the expected esteem and recognition, these individuals often resort to anger, condemnation, accusation, and domination.

Over time, such individuals will become increasingly more difficult. They will have become quite skilled and able to rationalize their brusque behavior with confusing spiritual language. Those who attempt to confront them without being prepared will walk away scratching their heads in confusion and will dismiss the thought that the person had Jezebellic tendencies — even though their initial discernment was correct.

If their strong will and disobedience are not dealt with, Jezebelites will rebel against any authority that does not agree with them. In addition, they will counsel others to rebel against pastoral authority — often presenting those who disagree with them as being spiritually blind or naive. This unchecked rebellion will open the door for other evil spirits to infiltrate them, their followers, or even an entire church. Consequently, a sudden, violent verbal attack may arise and be specifically targeted toward individuals who do not show loyalty or submission to the Jezebelite. Meanwhile, church members who seem indifferent or complacent to this rebellion will end up serving as pawns in a demonic game of win or lose. Tragically, the end result will usually be a church split.

A Spirit of Lawlessness

Lawlessness is a term used to describe people who are not restrained or controlled by the law, especially God's Word. In essence, all rebellion against God is lawlessness (1 John 3:4). Those who were responsible for the death of Jesus are characterized as lawless (Acts 2:23). The leader of the end-time rebellion, the Antichrist, is called the man of lawlessness (2 Thessalonians 2).

A spirit of lawlessness unleashes its attack on the Kingdom of God and drives individuals to rebel and oppose God's appointed leaders. This spirit inspires innuendos, rumors, lies, slander, manipulation, and control by creating schisms—or threatening to do so. Thus, whoever covertly challenges and slanders godly pastors and other ministries has violated God's established rules for His Kingdom. Such thinking is rebellion or sin.

> 1 John 3:4 Whosoever committeth sin transgresseth also the law: for sin is the transgression of the law.

Our omniscient God has foreknowledge of each pastor's theology, gifts, experiences, and personality. With infinite insight, God knows exactly how a pastor will carry out his or her ideas and plans for a church. A pastor's strengths will probably be evidenced first, followed by their weaknesses—neither of which surprise God. Thus, a pastor known to hurt people in relationships, whether knowingly or unknowingly, continues to be allowed to lead a church in spite of his or her weaknesses. God is patient, watching faithful pastors mature in character and gifting. Therefore if your pastor offends you, could it be God is using him or her to reveal your heart?

By speaking against God's established leaders, you are sowing seeds for your own destruction. Remember, Scripture tells us:

> 1 Timothy 5:19 Against an elder receive not an accusation, but before two or three witnesses.

The passage in Matthew 18 provides us with proper protocol to follow with any church member, including a pastor or a leader who has sinned or is in error.

> Matthew 18:15-18 Moreover if thy brother shall trespass against thee, go and tell him his fault between thee and him alone: if he shall hear thee, thou hast gained thy brother. But if he will not hear thee, then take with thee one or two more, that in the mouth of two or three witnesses every word may be established. And if he shall neglect to hear them, tell it unto the church: but if he neglect to hear the church, let him be unto thee as an heathen man and a publican. Verily I say unto you, Whatsoever ye shall bind on earth shall be bound in heaven: and whatsoever ye shall loose on earth shall be loosed in heaven.

Even if your pastor is angry and controlling like Saul, you must demonstrate a heart of David. You must refrain from taking the opportunity to "kill" God's leader (1 Samuel

24). David waited for God to intervene and deal with Saul. May it never be said of you, as it was of Absalom, that you stole the hearts of the people away from your pastor (2 Samuel 15:4-6).

Let God judge your pastor. If you judge him or her, God will be justified in saying, "Since men have taken action, I will step back." Thus, God will allow us to live with the results of our actions. In addition, by taking judgment into our own hands, we give demonic spirits a legal right to judge, hassle, harass, and come against us, simply because we have acted presumptively and have stepped out from under our covering. Therefore, it would be better to leave a church quietly than to speak against God's anointed.

Some people mistakenly think that because their gifts continue to be used, their actions are sanctioned by God. Remember what the Lord said:

> Matthew 7:21-23 Not every one that saith unto me, Lord, Lord, shall enter into the kingdom of heaven; but he that doeth the will of my Father which is in heaven. Many will say to me in that day, Lord, Lord, have we not prophesied in thy name? and in thy name have cast out devils? and in thy name done many wonderful works? And then will I profess unto them, I never knew you: depart from me, ye that work iniquity.

Some of us may think that because we are casting out demons, healing the sick, raising the dead, or prophesying accurately that it indicates God's stamp of approval. We may think we are within the will of God when we criticize our pastor, but God calls it lawlessness.

> Matthew 15:8 This people draweth nigh unto me with their mouth, and honoureth me with their lips; but their heart is far from me.

A heart dedicated and consecrated to the Lord honors the spiritual authority that God has established. A heart that rejects that authority allows lawlessness to influence perceptions and decisions.

Please understand that I am not saying we cannot question a spiritual leader who has authority over us. Inquiry is an important process of maturity. However, what we do after a disagreement is critical. If our conversation becomes covert, hidden, and malicious, then we are treading in the realm of lawlessness. Our actions depict lawlessness, especially if our intent is to remove that leader.

Since God has placed those in authority over us, we must be willing to submit to them. We should also make it a joy for them to watch over our souls.

> Hebrews 13:17, 18 Obey them that have the rule over you, and submit yourselves: for they watch for your souls, as they that must give account, that they may do it with joy, and not with grief: for that is unprofitable for you. Pray for us: for we trust we have a good conscience, in all things willing to live honestly.

Your willingness to submit to those in authority does not mean that you cannot have different ideas. You can experience great diversity in the midst of great unity. Once a course of action has been taken by leadership, however, you need to support their decision. If you find yourself questioning the direction taken by leadership, then seek another church that lines up with your ideals and calling. Furthermore, when making that change, do so with grace and humility, not with discord or strife. Otherwise, Scripture says it will be "unprofitable" for you.

> Proverbs 21:1 The king's heart is in the hand of the LORD, as the rivers of water: he turneth it whithersoever he will.

As you examine your own heart, ask yourself: Do you really believe God can turn your pastor's heart? Then why not step back and pray? We serve a faithful and just God, who is capable of bringing about changes in the heart of your pastor. If God shares your beliefs and priorities for the church, you may witness the pastor responding to divine revelation, which affects a change in his or her decisions and actions. If God does not bring about the changes you desire, perhaps the more important issue is you, not your pastor! Then you may want to ask yourself, "What is God trying to change in me?"

Accepting honest answers to questions such as these may point out areas in your life in which God desires change. In this process, you may benefit from a deeper understanding of yourself. You will also grow closer to the Lord, as you look to Him to influence your pastor.

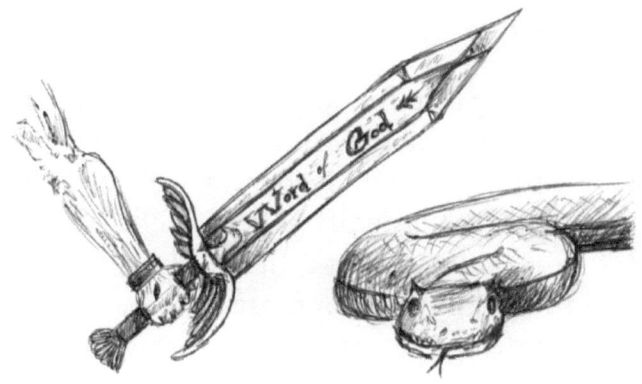

Chapter Eighteen
The Seduction of Jezebel

Jezebel has a way to hate someone but use seduction in a way to influence them. They love to flatter you into doing what they want you to do. The demonic spirit that inspired Herodias to murder John the Baptist (Matthew 14:6-11) was the Jezebel spirit. The spirit of Elijah that rested on John the Baptist had once again threatened and challenged the spirit of Jezebel. In pacifying her demands, he got what he wanted—sexual favors. She got what she wanted—the death of the prophet who threatened her rise to even greater power and authority.

Flattery is a primary tool used by someone influenced by the Jezebel spirit. Flattery is often used to pry open a door to endorsement by church leadership. Although offering sincere compliments that edify others in the Body of Christ are good, flattery differs in its motive. Flattery seeks to gain approval and recognition from those in authority. This spirit only gives in order to get, stealing authority and favor that would rightfully have been given to someone else.

Many pastors believe that a person with a strong prophetic gift automatically possesses the same level of moral character. However, a person operating with a Jezebel spirit — as well as an immature prophetic individual — can portray a very real and sometimes awesome prophetic gift, but remain; extremely weak in moral character as well as theology. In someone guided by a sophisticated Jezebel spirit, flattery will smooth over any differences between people. Flattery may be employed to portray profound admiration. It may seem to endorse the church's vision and direction. Such individuals will speak the same language as the pastor and leaders, but their motives will be to gain position and control. Stripped down, this strategy is "to conquer by joining" in spirit.

When flattery is being given by individuals with a Jezebel spirit, they may tell the pastor about the great things the pastor will accomplish, building up false hopes and false expectations about his or her future. Once this trap is set, the pastor will be told at precisely timed moments of weakness that there exists a danger to God's plans; someone or something is holding the pastor back. It may be the pastor's spouse, an elder or even another church member. This Jezebel may be heard praying for God to remove a "mystery" person so the pastor "can become all he or she is called to become." The praying one then guards the identity of the "mystery" person until confident of having a strong base of church support. Then, the identity of the person who is supposedly a threat will be revealed. This usually results in the mystery person's removal from a position of influence. These destructive maneuvers can bring incredible pressures on a pastor, who is provoked to arise and prove his or her worth and anointing to the church.

Flattery can also become a catalyst for causing division. Usually this ploy is accomplished through creating destructive "relational triangles." In a triangle, Jezebel will befriend person A and person B. However, Jezebel will slowly convince person A that person B does not like him or her. She will also convince person B that person A does not like him or her. Then, Jezebel will appear as a peacemaker who has a deep desire to see each one succeed. By fighting each one's gifting or wisdom against another's, this individual produces jealousy, strife, and contention—even in the strongest of relationships.

There is no satisfying the endless demands of a Jezebel spirit, because there is always something or someone standing in the way of their quest for power. This drives a pastor to discouragement, defeat, and despair. Over the years, I have watched many pastors retreat to another church rather than fight this battle.

Someone with a Jezebel spirit will seek to gain sympathy from many people, especially when confronted. Such individuals will claim they have been spiritually abused. They may use "words" to disarm arguments against them. If a pastor responds defensively to their discourse, he will only reinforce their accusations of being spiritually abused. If a pastor does not have a strong relationship with church leadership, he or she may become trapped in an irrational, unreasonable, or senseless situation.

An individual with a Jezebel spirit strategically affiliates with others in the Body who move in spiritual realms. Such individuals realize that those who are spiritual are looked upon favorably. Therefore, an individual with a Jezebel spirit shares that favor through strategic affiliation! Thus, this individual mounts his or her campaign to win popular and pastoral endorsement in his or her bid for growing influence.

> Proverbs 26:25 When he speaketh fair, believe him not: for there are seven abominations in his heart.

Tactics intended to frustrate the Kingdom of God will come easily to those operating with a Jezebel spirit. They seek recognition by trying to manipulate situations to their advantage. From deep within their soul, they will conjure up an unusual number of dreams and visions. They may also "borrow" dreams and revelations that God has given to others, presenting them as though God had given them the revelation. Or, they may enhance and embellish their own dreams to make them seem even more spectacular and impressive. Scripture offers an excellent perspective of God's view on this matter.

> Jeremiah 23:30-32 Therefore, behold, I am against the prophets, saith the LORD, that steal my words every one from his neighbour. Behold, I am against the prophets, saith the LORD, that use their tongues, and say, He saith. Behold, I am against them that prophesy false dreams, saith the LORD, and do tell them, and cause my people to err by their lies, and by their lightness; yet I sent them not, nor

commanded them: therefore they shall not profit this people at all, saith the LORD.

These individuals will carry false burdens from the Lord, hoping to appear spiritual. They may even believe they are speaking God's words, unable to recognize the deception under which they are operating. Once such a person gains an open door to the pastor, it is not uncommon for Jezebel to flood him or her with "revelation" that has supposedly been received from the Lord. Every situation will be subtly manipulated to cast a favorable light on the individual operating with a Jezebel spirit, thus bringing attention to the schemer rather than to the Lord. As this spirit's roots take deeper hold in the person's soul, righteous and redemptive fruit eventually become non-existent.

When an individual with a Jezebel spirit is put in a leadership position, he or she will try to create an impression of walking on a higher spiritual plane than most. Others may feel less spiritual or intimidated, when they are around this person. This ploy creates an emotional dependency in others. Feeling spiritually inferior, they will seek out the Jezebelite for spiritual guidance. Furthermore, if any question the Jezebelite's spirituality, they may experience harassment.

New believers are especially prone to this kind of subtle, but effective, intimidation. Some may choose to pull away from the person, but those who choose to stay will usually comply with the Jezebelite's demands rather than face being ostracized. Once joined to this spirit, believers who are weak or easily intimidated will find it difficult to remove themselves from the grip of the Jezebelite.

The integrity of the upright will guide them, but the perversity of the unfaithful will destroy them — Proverbs 11:3. they respond initially with false humility. This ploy will serve to further entrap you and convince you of their spirituality. However, this misleading meekness will be short lived. False humility is actually a mask for deeply rooted pride and presumption.

Once this false humility is discarded, this kind of person will proudly offer many "prophetic" promises. The Jezebelite will foretell of a great kingdom coming to the pastor. However, when these soulish predictions fail to materialize, a pastor's faith is deflated as hope deferred makes the heart sick (Proverbs 13:12). A dark cloud of depression may engulf the pastor, who begins to fight the urge to detach from his or her congregation.

By this time, the Jezebelite will have become entrenched in the church. Evicting this person or curtailing his or her usurped authority, would seem to bring about an exodus from the church, although it would save the church. If the pastor knew what to do, he or she no longer can summon the strength to fight back. If the pastor were to address the situation, he or she thinks that would risk making his or her leadership look foolish simply because the pastor was the one who placed the Jezebelite in the leadership position.

In leaving—or in threatening to leave—the Jezebelite usually discredits the pastor and claims the pastor is not as spiritual as people had thought. The Jezebelite may also maintain, "I'm just concerned for the people."

At this point, emotional blackmail ensues. Since a Jezebel spirit now holds the key to the emotional balance of the church, the individual will be able to confidently hold the pastor hostage. The pastor then becomes captive to obey directions from a demonic spirit. When this happens, a pastor may sense a sudden "call by God" to leave and shepherd another congregation in another city.

This situation will most likely recur until this pastor recognizes and admits to having an Ahab spirit and tolerating a Jezebel spirit. A similar fate awaits him or her at the new church. As long as these areas remain unhealed in the pastor's life, Satan will continue to exploit him or her by bringing another Jezebelite. God's severe mercy allows this tormentor to continually plague a pastor until he or she acknowledges, repents of, and finds healing from operating with an Ahab spirit.

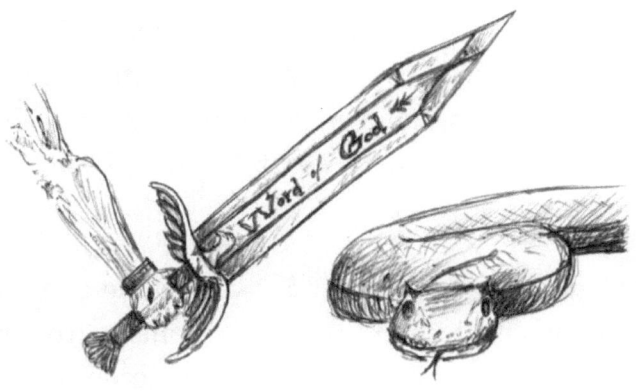

Chapter Nineteen
Evil Strategies of Jezebel

In order to overcome Jezebel we must recognize it's strategies. The spiritual world, with its opposing forces of good and evil, is a world that is in one sense more real and relevant than the natural realm we live in. The kingdom of darkness is waging all-out war against the Kingdom of God, and the Bible tells us that as spirit beings, we are caught in a struggle between these two realms. We struggle with "unseen entities" that manifest themselves through people by influencing their thinking—and thereby their actions. In these last days of the Church, the thrust of the enemy is mighty as he tries to establish strongholds in people's minds and seduce our world to come under the control of Jezebel and other evil principalities and powers.

To understand strongholds, we first have to know they exist. Rooted in our thinking and philosophies, strongholds are in us, not in the "heavenlies." They come through our perceptions and involve far more than our physical senses. What we see, hear, touch, taste and smell is by no means the limit of our existence. Our "natural man" needs these senses to interact with the natural world. The dimension that resides outside our natural senses, however—the realm consisting of spiritual entities, both good and evil—is impossible to interpret with the carnal mind. A carnal person relates only to things perceived by the physical senses. Being born-again, however, gives a person the ability to see beyond the physical. It causes us, because we are new creatures, to relate to the spiritual realm.

A strictly carnal mind cannot relate to the spiritual, yet many Christians are now in that condition. They have become blinded because they have adopted only a natural, sensual view of things. They do not recognize that they are influenced by spiritual forces, both good and evil, and they do not know that there are spiritual implications behind what goes on in their lives. Strongholds develop in them, yet they only look at the surface level. According to the writer of Hebrews, such believers are guilty of not exercising their spiritual senses, and thus remain carnal and immature in their perspective:

Hebrews 5:12-14 For when for the time ye ought to be teachers, ye have need that one teach you again which be the first principles of the oracles of God; and are become such as have need of milk, and not of strong meat. For every one that useth milk is unskilful in the word of righteousness: for he is a babe. But strong meat belongeth to them that are of full age, even those who by reason of use have their senses exercised to discern both good and evil.

When the enemy attempts to establish wrong ways of thinking—strongholds that hold people in spiritual captivity—carnal minds are the ideal place to start. That happens over and over again. For example, here in the United States, the kingdom of darkness strategically employs the fear of man to advocate political correctness. A huge concern over being seen as "politically correct" has paralyzed even committed Christians and has prevented them from speaking the truth. Through technology, the devil and his forces have access to the masses, and as in the days of Elijah, the majority submits and serves Baal because of the fear of man.

Political correctness has crippled many by appealing to the masses to compromise truth and erase all biblical standards. Liberal, heathen philosophers fill universities with a anti-God mindset. They operate under the Jezebel principality to shape the minds of the young—pure, innocent minds entering college, only to be told there is no God. The goal is to wash their minds of any moral standard and train them to be their own gods.

The United States is not the only culture prone to such influence, of course. The Jezebel principality operates around the world. The influence of Jezebel past and present in the world's systems is obvious.

Isaiah accurately prophesied the twisted venom that we see injected into the world's systems in our day:

> Isaiah 5:20 Woe unto them that call evil good, and good evil; that put darkness for light, and light for darkness; that put bitter for sweet, and sweet for bitter!

Alongside political correctness, a spirit of tolerance has moved right into the Church. While believers are to be long-suffering, we must also possess a pure desire to let the Holy Spirit have total preeminence. We are guilty of tolerating Jezebel, and like Elijah, we need the Holy Spirit to instill in us a hatred for the devil and his ways. We must yield to the Holy Spirit if we are to thwart the enemy's sinister strategies, because the influence of this Jezebel principality has never been eradicated from the Church. Instead, it has enjoyed an unholy reign and seems more entrenched than ever.

Certainly, one of the most insidious strategies Jezebel uses to accomplish its agenda is pornography. Ordinary men, as well as powerful leaders with mighty anointings, have become addicted. Usually they harbor a secret indulgence — one that keeps them powerless and ineffective. Burdened with guilt and shame, they are helpless to walk in victory.

When leaders with great potential become tolerant of Jezebel's nature, they also become spiritual eunuchs, robbed of their masculinity and proper sexual expression. They are enticed and then weakened, unable to function as authority-filled believers. These are respectable men, but because of secret sin, they have become tolerant of and sympathetic to

Jezebel's nature. Their prayers are those of feeble spiritual eunuchs instead of zealous, authority-filled believers.

More than ever, Satan is using "wickedness in the heavenly places" to deceive countless souls. Paul warned us that this battle is not with people but with the power of darkness:

> Ephesians 6:12 For we wrestle not against flesh and blood, but against principalities, against powers, against the rulers of the darkness of this world, against spiritual wickedness in high *places*.

If we are dealing with a Jezebel spirit, we must ask God to place in us an intolerance of all its activities. We must search our hearts and refuse to relinquish our power and authority as Christians by harboring unclean thoughts in our private lives. We must let the Holy Spirit work in us until the enemy can find no place of access in our lives.

> John 14:30 Hereafter I will not talk much with you: for the prince of this world cometh, and hath nothing in me.

There also needs to be nothing in us that invites Satan and his hordes, including Jezebel, to have their way. For many in the Old Testament, probably the most deceiving thing about Queen Jezebel was that she was religious and did religious things. She was the daughter of Ethbaal, whose name meant "with Baal." King Ahab married her against God's command, and she converted her husband into a Baal follower. The worship of Baal was idolatrous—essentially the worship of false gods and the work of one's own hands.

Queen Jezebel certainly lived up to her name. The name Jezebel is Phoenician in origin and specifically means without dwelling or habitation. This is true of those with her nature. A Jezebel spirit is independent; it cohabits with no one. The name can also be defined as "unmarried" or "uncommitted." Queen Jezebel was committed to her own self-will. Jezebel-type behavior clearly can be defined as the worship of self-will. People with a Jezebel spirit refuse to be team players or "cohabit" with anyone unless they can control and dominate the relationship.

Like Queen Jezebel of old, today's Jezebels can convincingly act "religious." They are always jockeying for a position in the Church.

Jezebel "calls herself a prophetess." Male or female, people with this spirit love to act religiously, and their motive in doing so is to gain power and control. Usually they will volunteer for anything at church—with the hidden agenda of gaining power and recognition. If they perceive that you are strong and cannot be controlled, they will not "cohabit" with you in a ministry. They will probably remove themselves from your presence and approach others to damage your reputation. If they perceive weakness on your part, they will come after you with a vengeance. They always exalt position over character. That is why humility is so greatly needed in the Church. The devil cannot do much with humility . . . but God can.

Individuals I have encountered who operate under a Jezebel spirit also do a lot of praying. But my question is, to whom are they praying? It appears as if they have created a god in their own minds who does not require them to follow Scriptures about agape love, humility and forgiveness. They frequently exempt themselves from extending forgiveness and proclaim themselves victims. They feel they do not need to forgive anyone because they are always the ones who have been hurt. They overlook the verse,

> Matthew 6:15 But if ye forgive not men their trespasses, neither will your Father forgive your trespasses.

They feel justified in living recklessly within a stronghold of pride, stubbornness, resentment and rebellion and excuse themselves from the "meaty" requirements of Scripture. From their distorted perspective, however, they probably believe that they are following Scripture and that it is everyone else who is not.

The Jezebel principality hates true prophets because they speak truth without compromise and give Jezebel no gray area in which to operate. In the New Covenant, this "prophetic voice" is in all believers:

> Acts 2:17 And it shall come to pass in the last days, saith God, I will pour out of my Spirit upon all flesh: and your sons and your daughters shall prophesy, and your young men shall see visions, and your old men shall dream dreams:

This is remarkable that the Lord is pouring out His Spirit on all flesh, but Jezebel hates the move of the Holy Spirit in the Church. That principality resists the revelation the move of the Spirit manifests—the witness of Jesus Christ and Him crucified.

All believers have the potential to prophesy, but not all stand in the office of a prophet. A prophet demands repentance and cuts away evil without compromise. Additionally, prophetic words come with creative power, which renders the enemy helpless. The Jezebel principality hates the uncompromising voice of a prophet. Jezebel spirits cannot accomplish their agenda with a prophet around. That is why people in the grip of a Jezebel spirit always try to bring division and strife in churches endeavoring to flow in the Holy Spirit. They will resist God's authority, promote their own agenda and sow seeds of discord to get as many people on their side as possible, undermining leadership. They will criticize a strong prophetic voice because it simply goes against their agenda.

In the Old Testament, no one rose up to oppose Queen Jezebel except the prophet Elijah. Scripture records that they were always in conflict. Jezebel was Elijah's archenemy. Her hatred and malice toward him was limitless, and she devoted much time to trying to destroy him and his message.

Jezebel and Ahab's Baal worship involved worshiping false gods—the work of human hands. It also included child sacrifice, perverted heterosexual relationships and homosexuality. The prophet Elijah had enough of it! Willing to confront evil, he called for the prophets who ate at Jezebel's table to come forth:

> 1 Kings 18:19 Now therefore send, and gather to me all Israel unto mount Carmel, and the prophets of Baal four hundred and fifty, and the prophets of the groves four hundred, which eat at Jezebel's table.

Then he challenged everyone present,

> 1 Kings 18:23, 24 Let them therefore give us two bullocks; and let them choose one bullock for themselves, and cut it in pieces, and lay it on wood, and put no fire under: and I will dress the other bullock, and lay it on wood, and put no fire under: And call ye on the name of your gods, and I will call on the name of the LORD: and the God that answereth by fire, let him be God. And all the people answered and said, It is well spoken.

The false prophets called on their god to consume the sacrifice, but nothing happened. They leaped about the altar and cried aloud and cut themselves until their blood gushed out (verses 26–29), but still nothing happened.

Elijah repaired the altar of the Lord and called upon Him. When the fire of God fell, it "consumed the burnt sacrifice, and the wood and the stones and the dust, and it licked up the water that was in the trench." When the people saw the power of God, "they fell on their faces; and they said, 'The Lord, He is God! The Lord, He is God!'" (verses 38–39).

Next, Elijah commanded, "Seize the prophets of Baal! Do not let one of them escape!"

(1 Kings 18:40). So the people seized them, and Elijah brought them to the Brook Kishon and executed them. Elijah's actions were more than simply a means of destroying false prophets. Elijah carried them out in such a way that they

brought repentance to the people of God for ever following them. The nation had to repent and turn back to God! A true prophetic anointing does not just tickle ears but challenges people to turn and repent.

The battle between Jezebel and Elijah was over control of the people. If we are not people of decision, we are in grave danger of falling under the spell of a Jezebel spirit. People with Jezebel spirits want control and are good at getting their way. When you oppose them, you will pay a price. That is why so many seem to look the other way rather than boldly dealing with conflict.

After Elijah killed the prophets of Baal, Ahab renounced his authority to Jezebel.

> 1 Kings 19:1 And Ahab told Jezebel all that Elijah had done, and withal how he had slain all the prophets with the sword.

Then he left the situation in her hands. Furious, she put a death threat on Elijah:

> 1 Kings 19:2 Then Jezebel sent a messenger unto Elijah, saying, So let the gods do *to me*, and more also, if I make not thy life as the life of one of them by to morrow about this time.

It is perplexing that Elijah, a mighty man of God who had just stood against 850 false prophets, ran for his life from one woman!

> 1 Kings 19:3, 4 And when he saw that, he arose, and went for his life, and came to Beersheba, which belongeth to Judah, and left his servant there. But he himself went a day's journey into the wilderness, and came and sat down under

a juniper tree: and he requested for himself that he might die; and said, It is enough; now, O LORD, take away my life; for I am not better than my fathers.

Jezebel used intimidation with great effectiveness—and with a vengeance. In Elijah's case, she used verbal threats so intimidating that Elijah responded to fear instead of to God.

Jezebels love to project a false sense of power, using fear and intimidation to cloud and confuse the minds of those they desire to oppress. How frequently such spirits try to use their influence! Examples in church might be those who tell the pastor, "If you take this action, we will withhold our tithe," or leaders who tell those under them, "Submit to me or you won't have a spiritual covering." In a family setting, one might hear from a spouse, "If you don't see it my way, you can sleep in another bed," or "I'll leave and take the kids with me." In the business world, a manager might threaten, "You can forget about a promotion," or a disgruntled worker might threaten, "I'll sue this company until you go out of business." These are all improper channels through which controlling people use illegitimate authority to project power that is not really theirs.

All of us who have felt the rage of a Jezebel spirit directed our way through another person can identify with Elijah. We are in good company! Elijah was temporarily influenced by fear, which caused him to be bound by discouragement and despair. He was paralyzed by Jezebel's projected "power," but God delivered him.

Jezebel's threats so intimidated and blinded Elijah that from his perspective, it seemed that not one other person was left who was devoted to God. When God confronted Elijah, the prophet said,

> 1 Kings 19:10 And he said, I have been very jealous for the LORD God of hosts: for the children of Israel have forsaken thy covenant, thrown down thine altars, and slain thy prophets with the sword; and I, even I only, am left; and they seek my life, to take it away.

A Jezebel spirit wants you to feel abandoned and surrender to hopelessness, as Elijah momentarily did. It wants you to lose your identity, authority and self-worth, and it wants you to give in to self-pity and a victim mentality. It can distort and twist your perspective so that you may think you are the only one standing up for the Lord.

The Jezebel principality may have caused over ten million Hebrews in Elijah's time to bow down to Baal, but God quickly clarified Elijah's perspective. He told the prophet,

> 1 Kings 19:18 Yet I have left *me* seven thousand in Israel, all the knees which have not bowed unto Baal, and every mouth which hath not kissed him.

Elijah was not as alone as Jezebel wanted him to think, and neither are you and I!

Jezebel also desires to paralyze the prophetic flow of God. It had paralyzed Elijah, who surrendered to self-pity. Self-pity is clearly a conscious resignation in which a person surrenders to a victim mentality. When you see yourself as a victim, you literally enter into sin with Jezebel because you are not offering any resistance. For example, in my society, those who do not stand up against the pro-abortion philosophy and other liberal and worldly standards are in effect entering into sin with Jezebel. Many compromise and go along with the pro-abortion (or pro-choice) philosophy and other liberal views, embracing a politically correct standard because they fear the reaction of their peers. Do not enter into such sin with Jezebel—resist! Embrace the truth instead. The way to stand against a Jezebel spirit is through prayer, a commitment to the truth and a willingness to confront lies.

Let's take a look at the differences between Elijah's spirit and Jezebel's. One ushers in the power of God and brings repentance and change, as the prophet Elijah did. The other puts on a false religious front and tries to control through intimidation and deceit, as Queen Jezebel did.

Elijah demands repentance. Jezebel hates repentance. Elijah demands righteousness. Jezebel opposes righteousness. Elijah speaks freedom. Jezebel desires control. Elijah demands humility. Jezebel appeals to pride. Elijah speaks God's ways. Jezebel uses deceit and systems of witchcraft. Elijah wants God on the throne. Jezebel wants self on the throne.

God hates the Jezebel principality and will bring judgment upon it. Jezebel spirits destroy families, churches, businesses and relationships. Plainly, they destroy lives. Something that has always troubled me, however, is the way that those who yield to a Jezebel spirit seem to get away with it in the here and now. I have never understood that, yet I do believe that God in His mercy gives a person time to repent (Revelation 2:21).

Yet I also know that as individuals, churches and leadership, we all have to take a stronger stand against Jezebel. God is often waiting for someone to stand up to a spirit of Jezebel—to confront it. Many succumb to an Ahab spirit, though, and simply turn their heads away from a Jezebel's tactics. They reason that, after all, he or she is religious and works hard in the Church. Many who are confronted by such a person follow the way of King Ahab— which at first seems like the easy way. One of the greatest weaknesses among leaders facing Jezebel is their fear of confrontation. They want peace without paying the price of confronting the manipulative and controlling tactics of a Jezebel.

Jehu was an instrument God could use. He had no fear of confrontation. His name, Jehu, means "Jehovah is He." As the newly anointed king of Israel, Jehu was given a clear command from the Lord through the prophet Elisha:

> 2 Kings 9:7 And thou shalt smite the house of Ahab thy master, that I may avenge the blood of my servants the prophets, and the blood of all the servants of the LORD, at the hand of Jezebel.

Sent to fulfill the word of the Lord, Jehu killed King Jehoram and King Ahaziah, and then he went to confront Jezebel.

When Jehu arrived on the scene to deal with Jezebel and the others as God had commanded, the watchmen who spotted him reported that "the driving is like the driving of Jehu the son of Nimshi, for he drives furiously!" (2 Kings 9:20). Jehu was on a mission of zero tolerance. Like him, those who deal with a spirit of Jezebel must do so without compromise. To confront Jezebel and get results, we must be as furiously determined as Jehu was. We must be aggressive "drivers."

Jehu did not try to pacify that foul spirit of Jezebel. The first horseman who met Jehu coming into the city asked him, "Thus says the king: 'Is it peace?'" Jehu replied, "What have you to do with peace? Turn around and follow me" (2 Kings 9:18). And he made the same reply to the second horseman who asked him. Then King Joram asked, "Is it peace, Jehu?" Notice Jehu's answer: "What peace, as long as the harlotries of your mother Jezebel and her witchcraft are so many?" (2 Kings 9:22).

Even Jezebel asked Jehu if it was peace, using her seductive tactics to try to influence him:

> 2 Kings 9:30, 31 And when Jehu was come to Jezreel, Jezebel heard *of it;* and she painted her face, and tired her head, and looked out at a window. And as Jehu entered in at the gate, she said, *Had* Zimri peace, who slew his master?

There was no room for compromise in Jehu. He refused to be seduced into a false peace. Like Jehu, we must not yield to the temptation of comfort and false peace while the Jezebel principality runs rampant in the world. We must refuse to be peacekeepers and instead become peacemakers. We must stand firmly on God's side and realize that we are dealing with an evil being. Although we must be compassionate toward the person in its clutches, we must deal it a death blow. To do so, we have no choice but to allow the Holy Spirit to show us where we are sympathetic and tolerant to the demonic force of Jezebel—not only in church, but in our everyday lives.

Like Jezebel of old, people with a Jezebel spirit love to surround themselves with those who can be emasculated and easily controlled. Jezebels will feed their victims with spiritual pride to establish an ungodly soul tie and win their confidence. They will befriend and support controllable leaders— encouraging other followers to get behind a weak leader susceptible to being controlled. Jezebels do not care whom God assigns to a position; they just want someone in power who will take their advice. As I said earlier, they will not "cohabit" or "dwell" with anyone unless they can dominate the relationship. Many times they outwardly will feign servant-likeness or submissiveness, but inwardly they will harbor the motive of gaining the advantage.

I find it most interesting that Queen Jezebel had eunuchs at her side, men she had stripped of their manhood and authority. Many since their time have become eunuchs—slaves—to this demonic force. Jezebel spirits love to connect with those who have an Ahab behavior—people pleasers without a backbone, who are willing to abdicate their authority and become passive and nonassertive. It was a welcome vindication to Jezebel's eunuchs, no doubt, to throw down their controlling queen. Heaven must have applauded their response to Jehu, who looked up at the window where Jezebel stood and asked with great authority, "Who is on my side? Who?" Two or three eunuchs looked out at him to indicate that they would take a stand against her (2 Kings 9:32). Jehu immediately commanded them, "Throw her down." They threw her down, and "some of her blood spattered on the wall and on the horses; and he trampled her underfoot" (2 Kings 9:33).

There is such significance in this. Those men whom the queen had castrated, humiliated and rendered powerless became instruments of her destruction. Sweet vindication! Victims of this treacherous principality must rise up in the power of God and be ruthless against it, just as these eunuchs were. Let God use you as an instrument in throwing a Jezebel spirit of control down. We must stop compromising with Jezebel and cling to the purpose of God. When dealing with a person manifesting a Jezebel spirit, many believers make the mistake of being far too easy on it. We lack victory if we live in false peace where a spirit of Jezebel is concerned. Just as Jehu commanded Queen Jezebel to be thrown down, we must be aggressive, not soft. We must be ruthless, dealing it a deathblow without sympathy. God is going to let us cast this foul spirit down the way Queen Jezebel's eunuchs cast her down. We cannot negotiate with a "terrorist" Jezebel spirit. Although we can love the person in its grip, we must hate Jezebel and its behavior.

It is interesting to note how the word of the Lord came to pass concerning Jezebel's life: "And concerning Jezebel the Lord also spoke, saying, 'The dogs shall eat Jezebel by the wall of Jezreel'" (1 Kings 21:23). The name Jezreel means "God soweth." God sowed a disaster plan against Jezebel and her wickedness. After the eunuchs threw her down, Jehu used his horse to trample her underfoot. He later commanded the eunuchs to go and bury her because she was a king's daughter, but they could not accord her the dignity of a grave:

> 2 Kings 9:35-37 And they went to bury her: but they found no more of her than the skull, and the feet, and the palms of *her* hands. Wherefore they came again, and told him. And he said, This *is* the word of the LORD, which he spake by his servant Elijah the Tishbite, saying, In the portion of Jezreel shall dogs eat the flesh of Jezebel: And the carcase of Jezebel shall be as dung upon the face of the field in the portion of Jezreel; *so* that they shall not say, This *is* Jezebel.

God desires to bring eternal judgment on the Jezebel principality. Its influence in the Church must end. God is raising up those who will be militant against it, not only by becoming unyielding and assertive, but by living in full repentance, walking in total humility and loving truth more than popularity and reputation. Just as Jehu's commission was to rid the kingdom of the defiling, demoralizing influences of Ahab and Jezebel, a call is going forth today to those who are willing to stand without compromise and confront those same apostate spirits that need to be removed from the Church.

In the New Testament, John the Baptist confronted King Herod and told him some things he did not want to hear; for example, "It is not lawful for you to have your brother's wife" (Mark 6:18). After that, a spirit of Jezebel began operating through his wife, Herodias, who brainstormed the idea of murder: "Therefore Herodias held it against him and wanted to kill him, but she could not" (verse 19).

A Jezebel spirit is strong and seeks what it wants, waiting for an opportunity. No wonder the Bible warns us to give no place (opportunity) to the devil (see Ephesians 4:27). When Herod gave a feast for his dignitaries, Herodias's daughter came in and danced. He was so pleased with her dance that he told her,

> Mark 6:22, 23 And when the daughter of the said Herodias came in, and danced, and pleased Herod and them that sat with him, the king said unto the damsel, Ask of me whatsoever thou wilt, and I will give *it* thee. And he sware unto her, Whatsoever thou shalt ask of me, I will give *it* thee, unto the half of my kingdom.

So the girl asked her mother what she should request, and Herodias, in true Jezebel fashion said, "The head of John the Baptist!" (verse 24).

Herodias could not receive correction and seek repentance; therefore, she had to destroy the one who spoke truth. She used her own daughter to do the dastardly deed. A Jezebel spirit typically gets someone else to do its dirty work.

The same type of spirit that desired to destroy Elijah was clearly responsible for cutting off the head of John the Baptist. The same Holy Spirit who was on Elijah rested on John the Baptist, manifesting the same passion and focus. God said of John, "He will also go before Him in the spirit and power of Elijah" (Luke 1:17). Jesus explained to His disciples regarding John, "He is Elijah who is to come" (Matthew 11:14). John also was a preacher of repentance. When he confronted the sin of King Herod and Herodias, she held it against him and wanted him killed—the same attitude Queen Jezebel displayed toward Elijah. History repeated itself.

The Jezebel principality hates a prophet, because the prophetic voice demands repentance and a surrender of self-will. A prophet calls people to the cross. Jezebel hates the cross because of the repentance and restoration it represents. Jesus proclaimed, "Elijah is coming first and will restore all things" (Matthew 17:11). Malachi also prophesied,

> Behold, I will send you Elijah the prophet. Before the coming of the great and dreadful day of the Lord. And he will turn. The hearts of the fathers to the children, And the hearts of the children to their fathers, Lest I come and strike the earth with a curse.

I believe that today God is raising up a Body of passionate believers who are not afraid to confront Jezebel and who will operate in the spirit of Elijah, preparing the Church for the return of the Lord. As part of that Body, our strategy must be one of zero tolerance. We must always stand against Jezebel and expose its tactics, wherever it operates—in the Church, the home, the marriage or the workplace.

Some might be wondering at this point why, instead of all this confronting and exposing and standing against the principality of Jezebel, we cannot just cast out the evil spirits that so cunningly grip people's lives? After all, as Christians we have authority over demons. Here lies the problem: Although the demonic influence of Jezebel flows through a person, that person is also operating out of his or her own self-centered and stubborn flesh and functioning out of an urepentant human will. In other words, we cannot cast out the flesh—we can only stop Jezebel's influence, and that only briefly at best unless the person is willing to change his or her long-standing patterns of behavior.

The learned behavior of Jezebels is deeply rooted, and they enjoy the taste of power (although distorted) that a Jezebel spirit provides. Their personalities and demeanor often have been formed out of a lifetime of distorted thinking and being in control. Jezebel-type characteristics are so firmly entrenched in their personalities that "casting out the demon" does not address the whole problem.

It is very important to remember that in our warfare against such things, we do not "cast out" principalities—we wrestle against them!

> Ephesians 6:12 For we wrestle not against flesh and blood, but against principalities, against powers, against the rulers of the darkness of this world, against spiritual wickedness in high *places*.

Many misinterpret these verses to mean that "flesh and blood" and principalities, powers and rulers are mutually exclusive. In the context of these verses, however, they are not! In the same way that a person presents his or her body "a living sacrifice, holy, acceptable to God" (Romans 12:1), he or she also yields to a spirit of darkness. Both conditions require a decision on the part of the individual, and all spirits, both holy and unholy, influence people and use "flesh and blood" through which to manifest.

We defeat the influence of lies and deception coming from Satan and his forces by opening ourselves to the truth of God's Word. By speaking truth in love with the Word of God, we expose unholy principalities and cast down their strongholds in people's minds. The only way to get rid of the influence of Jezebel on someone is to bring truth against the deception the person has embraced for so long. The person must move toward repentance, but those with a Jezebel spirit usually run from repentance. Rarely will people under a Jezebel spirit truly repent and take personal responsibility for wrongdoing. Honestly, in my years of ministry I have rarely seen a Jezebel delivered. Sometimes the person becomes temporarily remorseful, but soon he or she goes back to using controlling tactics. I am not saying that there is absolutely no hope for someone bound by a spirit of Jezebel.

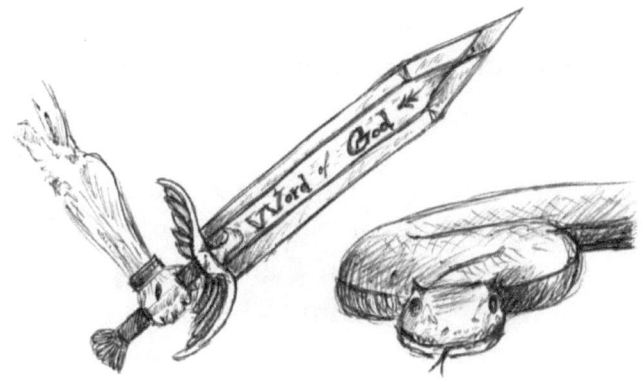

Chapter Twenty

Destroying the Spirit of Jezebel

A large part of apostolic ministry is spiritual warfare. In building the church, we will have to contend with spirits that want to destroy the church. In this books I expose the spirit of Jezebel.

I want to share with you a revelation of Christ given to me to help build the church. It is a revelation of Christ as "a eunuch for the kingdom's sake". It will be done in several pages, but I am sure if you read each one they will help you to defeat the covenant breaking spirit of Jezebel operating around your life and possibly attacking the very church you worship in.

In short, the spirit of Jezebel is not just some bossy woman who seizes the authority (responsibility) of her husband, but a spirit of satan that teaches people to break their covenant love relationships. The kingdom of God is all about covenant relationships! This misunderstanding of Jezebel has caused much hurt in the body of Christ and devalued the role of women in the service of God in the house of God. The spirit of Jezebel, in a man, is far worse at times in breaking covenant and destroying the church. The way God destroyed Jezebel in her day, is still the way to defeat this destructive spirit in our generation today.

Apostles empowering and encouraging the priestly ministry of covenant keeping unmarried people... can and will destroy this spirit. The spirit of Jezebel is not simply going away. Apostolic believers must enforce the victory Christ, the covenant keeping, covenant defending Son won at Calvary.

In fact every ministry called by Christ to function in reconciling people in covenant relationship to God will have to contend with this spirit that is behind teaching people to break covenant. I believe the Holy Spirit placed, in the context of the literal defeat of queen Jezebel, keys to defeat this spirit today in our generation.

I believe demonic spirits (for example, principalities) are high-ranking spirits that attempt to shape principles of people away from the principles, values and statutes of scripture. The principles of the Word of God when practiced should produce a person who values covenant love, one who reconciles relationships and a redeemer of people. All things pertaining to the blessings of God surround being joined to God by His words. Words that are associated with covenant are joined, attached, alliances, faithful, loyal, committed, devoted, these are the things the spirit of Jezebel fights against. In fact, this spirit looks for covenants to break up!

I want to look at the ministry of the Christ on another level (the eunuch for the kingdom's sake) and explore what I believe is a revelation to practically destroy a spirit sent from hell to keep us from Kohat and Hebron, it is the spirit called (Jezebel). I want to offer another perspective on the function of this vile spirit. I want to show you how it can be defeated from our position at the right hand of the Father.

First, I want to introduce you to the gift or function of service that God has raised up to defeat the "spirit of Jezebel". It is called the priesthood working with the gift of apostle.

> There is a three-fold anointing revealed and typified through the priestly line of Levi:
> 1. Levi… the grace to be attached (singular)
> 2. The ability to function corporately (as a congregation) and
> 3. Then on to Hebron the place of joining, alliances and confederations.

It is a priestly anointing. We have heard on several occasions teaching about the Melchisedek priesthood through the course of this school and my heart continues to leap as God has led me to discover more of the ramifications of understanding this order. We will take a practical look at a potent place for all saints to develop in this order.

God our Father has always wanted a people joined to Himself. From the outset of liberating Israel from Egypt, God had a purpose for Israel.

> Exodus 19:3-6 And Moses went up unto God, and the LORD called unto him out of the mountain, saying, Thus shalt thou say to the house of Jacob, and tell the children of Israel; Ye have seen what I did unto the Egyptians, and *how* I bare you on eagles' wings, and brought you unto myself. Now therefore, if ye will obey my voice indeed, and keep my covenant, then ye shall be a peculiar treasure unto me above all people: for all the earth *is* mine: And ye shall be unto me a kingdom of priests, and an holy nation. These *are* the words which thou shalt speak unto the children of Israel.
>
> 1 Peter 2:1-5 Wherefore laying aside all malice, and all guile, and hypocrisies, and envies, and all evil speakings, As newborn babes, desire the sincere milk of the word, that ye may grow thereby: If so be ye have tasted that the Lord *is* gracious. To whom coming, *as unto* a living stone, disallowed indeed of men, but chosen of God, *and* precious, Ye also, as lively stones, are built up a spiritual house, an holy priesthood, to offer up spiritual sacrifices, acceptable to God by Jesus Christ.
>
> 1 Peter 2:9, 10 But ye *are* a chosen generation, a royal priesthood, an holy nation, a peculiar people; that ye should shew forth the praises of him who hath called you out of darkness into his marvellous light: Which in time past *were* not a people, but *are* now the people of God: which had not obtained mercy, but now have obtained mercy.

It is very clear from looking at the scriptures above, the eternal intent of the Lord. God has always purposed, a company of sons who function from a king- priest dimension. But also from the very outset there has been an attempt to stop this covenant relationship by seducing humanity into fornication.

The war being fought in the kingdom is covenant vs. fornication. Let the warfare begin!

Adam functioned as king/priest, Melchisedek functioned as a king/priest, David functioned as king/priest, Christ functioned as a king/priest, the Body of Christ is supposed to function in the earth as kings and priests!

Without seeing Christ's ministry in the earth through the eyes of the priesthood is to miss a key component in covenant living. The component I am speaking of is the power of being joined. This is the power that defeats Jezebel.

I want to suggest a new look at Christ's ministry in the earth and show you the characteristics built in it to overcome the traits that threaten Hebron (alliances and covenant). It is the ability to defeat the spirit of Jezebel by the apostolic anointing covenanting with the unmarried priesthood and throwing her down!

In looking at the kingdom of God and while discussing the most lethal issues and aspects concerning covenant, Jesus releases a saying so potent with protection, many have been afraid to touch it. I believe our generation has been blessed to have this truth opened. We will use it to destroy the works of the devil against Christ's church.

> Matthew 19:12 For there are some eunuchs, which were so born from *their* mother's womb: and there are some eunuchs, which were made eunuchs of men: and there be eunuchs, which have made themselves eunuchs for the

kingdom of heaven's sake. He that is able to receive *it*, let him receive *it*.

Jesus is defending a covenant perspective against those who were not in covenant with the words of His Father fornication. As He is doing so, He speaks from an understanding that signals fierce loyalty. Jesus begins to discuss the ministry of the "eunuch for the kingdom's sake"; covenant keeping, covenant defending ministry.

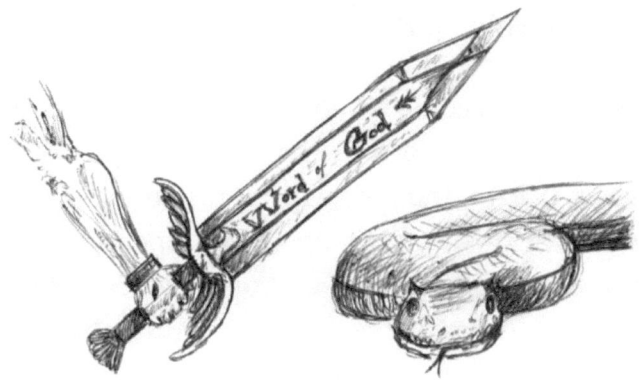

Chapter Twenty One

Dealing With Jezebel?

When we deal with Jezebel, we must move them to repentance. This can be difficult. We have to realize that true deliverance is needed. Can people with a Jezebel spirit come to repentance? Yes, absolutely. First, however, they must recognize their behavioral patterns and controlling motives and ruthlessly be willing to face the truth. They must let God crucify their flesh. Then, to be permanently set free, they must subject the flesh and all its patterns to the Holy Spirit daily.

Freedom can come when someone who is not afraid of a reaction confronts a person who has a Jezebel spirit. Confronted in firmness and love, the person may recognize that spirit and its effects, and he or she may respond by repenting and seeking deliverance. The only way to get rid of a Jezebel spirit is to bring truth to the one under deception. Truth always outdoes deception. Without a confrontation with the truth, people under the influence of Jezebel have no motive to change and will continue in the controlling lifestyle that has been their pattern for so long.

Both deception and truth have the ability to take root in the human heart, thereby guiding our actions. Deception can be powerful and enticing. When a person—any person, believer or unbeliever—is unwilling to search out and embrace the truth, he or she will always be bound by deception. But when deception is brought into the light, the enemy's lies are revealed. God's Word brings revelation and freedom. The light of the Word illuminated in the human heart is what casts out darkness. As Jesus said,

> John 8:32 And ye shall know the truth, and the truth shall make you free.

Perhaps instead of facing another person who has a Jezebel spirit, you are facing yourself and have noticed some controlling tendencies that raise warning flags in you. After reading the stories in this book and thinking about the behavioral traits we have listed, you may see yourself in some of these pages and be asking, Am I the one influenced by this spirit? How can I be free of Jezebel? These are important questions to start with on the road to repentance. It is good for you as a believer to ask yourself some hard questions. They can be a tremendous step toward liberation from a controlling way of life.

If you are wondering whether you have opened yourself up to the influence of Jezebel, here are some other questions to carefully consider:

> 1. Have you ever taken part in forcing a pastor out of his position?
> 2. Are you jealous of other people by nature?
> 3. Have you ever slandered someone to make yourself look good?
> 4. Have you ever manipulated others by putting guilt on them? Have you ever used anger or tears to get others to do something you want?
> 5. Have you found yourself in constant conflict with authority throughout your life? For example, when you have changed churches or jobs, have you left thinking, That person was the worst pastor (or worst boss) ever? Have you allowed yourself to feel resentful toward people who hold a position of leadership or authority?
> 6. Have you ever tried to get rid of someone else in order to set yourself up?

These sins do not mean that you are a Jezebel, yet if you have taken part in them or others like them, you may be manifesting some of Jezebel's characteristics. They are a fruit of the flesh, and you need to get them out of the way in order to go on in your spiritual life and avoid the judgment such sin always brings.

How do you get Jezebel's influence and characteristics out of your life? There is nothing like true repentance to render a spirit of Jezebel inoperative! Repentance brings freedom. Praying Psalm 51 for a period of time can be very beneficial and powerful. Ask the Lord to help you focus on specific verses and areas of your life in which you need to repent and change—verses like "Create in me a clean heart, O God, and renew a steadfast spirit within me" (verse 10).

> Psalms 138:6 Though the LORD *be* high, yet hath he respect unto the lowly: but the proud he knoweth afar off.

From His high and lofty position, the Lord observes every heart. He is not looking for the boastful and arrogant, but for the humble and contrite. Although He is Creator of all the universe, He is looking for the spiritually bankrupt whose hearts are crushed.

> Isaiah 66:2 For all those *things* hath mine hand made, and all those *things* have been, saith the LORD: but to this *man* will I look, *even* to *him that is* poor and of a contrite spirit, and trembleth at my word.

The key characteristic of the humble and contrite is that they respond with reverence when they hear God's Word. What does the Lord desire to do with them? He wants to bring spiritual restoration:

> Psalms 138:7 Though I walk in the midst of trouble, thou wilt revive me: thou shalt stretch forth thine hand against the wrath of mine enemies, and thy right hand shall save me.

The God of compassion wants to restore the crushed.

> Psalms 145:18 The LORD *is* nigh unto all them that call upon him, to all that call upon him in truth.

> Psalms 147:3 He healeth the broken in heart, and bindeth up their wounds.

> Psalms 113:7 He raiseth up the poor out of the dust, *and* lifteth the needy out of the dunghill;

Even if you have opened the door to a Jezebel spirit in the past, you can close the door now and be free—if you are determined to walk in true repentance and to change. No matter where you are spiritually, these truths are the beginning of your restoration.

When believers surrender totally to the person and nature of Christ, it terrifies and cripples the power of darkness more than anything else. To be Christ-like is to exercise a powerful weapon against the enemy, because, after all, Satan and the Jezebel principality are specifically opposed to the nature of Christ.

To have a disdain and intolerance for all types of Jezebel's influence, there must be consistency in our lives as believers. We must pursue the Lord until there are no grounds on which the enemy can point a finger at us (John 14:30). For example, many times we who rejoice and worship the Lord in church come home later and watch immoral entertainment on television. When we tolerate Jezebel's influence in our private lives, we give it inroads into the sanctuary of our lives. Our inconsistent behavior does not fool God. As Revelation 2:20 says,

> Revelations 2:20 Notwithstanding I have a few things against thee, because thou sufferest that woman Jezebel, which calleth herself a prophetess, to teach and to seduce my servants to commit fornication, and to eat things sacrificed unto idols.

By tolerating Jezebel, we greatly hinder the flow of God's power in our lives and our effectiveness for Him. The strategy of the devil is not just to tempt us to sin, but to bring us into shame so that we become emasculated and weakened in our authority to resist him. The bottom line is that we must equip ourselves with new resolve to war against Jezebel. Rather than sulking in condemnation over sins we have so easily given in to, we need to war aggressively against Jezebel and shake off all its influence.

To be Christ-like there is nothing in us that a Jezebel spirit fears more than prayer. Real prayer is simply praying what is on the mind of God. Strategic prayer is coming into alignment with God's thoughts and praying specifically therein. Many are bound to praying their own agenda. There is no power in that. True intercessory prayer is praying God's agenda. That kind of prayer throws a wrecking ball on the strategies of Jezebel and extracts its influence from the souls of men.

Intercessory prayer turns people's hearts away from immorality, bringing true repentance and godliness. True, fervent prayer causes hearts to change from pride and loftiness to repentance and humility. Nothing brings a greater death blow to the principality of Jezebel and its host of fallen spirits. Pray according to God's Word. Jezebel no doubt fears most the spoken Word of God as it comes forth with creative power.

What can you and I do about Jezebel? How can we walk in victory over this principality and its evil spirits, which infiltrate any open doors people provide in the weakness of their flesh? There are several things I believe all of us can do to walk in victory. I want to list here some mandatory steps you and I can take, both to confront this spirit of hell and to minimize its influence in our lives, in our families and in our churches. These steps will help protect us from coming under the grip of a Jezebel spirit and trying to control others. These steps will also help us avoid allowing someone already under the control of Jezebel to manipulate and abuse us.

1. Develop and strengthen your inner life. Our battle is not against flesh and blood, so time alone with God building up the inner man is foremost. Meditate on the truth, pray and learn to stand firm. Listen to the still, small voice of the Father. Get His wisdom!

2. Forgive and bless your parents and every authority figure who has wronged you. This step is major if you need healing from wounds of the past and protection from spiritual attack.

3. Seek the baptism in the Holy Spirit. This power is available to every Christian. It is unwise for any believer not to take advantage of this mighty gift of God in these evil days.

4. Seek inner healing and deliverance. Everyone has been wounded by life and subjected to demonic attacks and the formation of strongholds. To the degree that you experience true freedom through inner healing and deliverance from demons is the degree you will walk in victory over Jezebel.

5. Ask God to show you generational patterns and possible curses; then ask Him to break them. Patterns that were modeled for you and curses passed down from another generation need not remain part of your life.

6. Understand and apply the power of the cross, which can deliver us from ourselves. The Lord Jesus crucified your selfishness and self-centeredness on the cross. Ask Him to reveal every area of your flesh that you have not reckoned dead, and submit those areas to Him (Romans 6:12).

7. Be alert to the patterns of Jezebel in your life and in those around you. Ask God for discernment, and use righteousness judgment when you encounter people controlled by a Jezebel spirit—make sure you deal with your own issues first, not being a forgetful hearer, but rather a doer of the Word (James 1:25).

8. If you have been in the grip of Jezebel, expect warfare as you seek deliverance into a new walk. This spirit wants to destroy you. Your daily battle for freedom may not involve "knockout" capabilities, but rather inch-by-inch, point-counterpoint progress. Patterns of behavior that have long been in development may not necessarily change overnight, but they will change as you submit yourself to Christ.

9. Forgive as quickly and as deeply as you can. Unforgiveness is an open door to the enemy!

10. Bless and do not curse; do not return evil for

evil. You break curses by blessing, giving thanks in everything and knowing that God works everything for your good.

11. Daily lay down everything in your life at the feet of Jesus. Only what is spiritual will pass beyond the grave.

12. Use this book as a battle plan. I trust there are priceless nuggets here that will sharpen your sword and open your eyes.

13. Be keenly aware of how subtle Jezebel's seduction of your spirit, mind and body can be. Jezebel is crafty and can easily play on your senses and emotions.

14. Learn to walk in agape love. Worldly, carnal people and many Christians walk in a selfish "What's in it for me?" kind of love. Ask God to teach you how to walk in, live in and breathe in His love working in and through you. You will never be the same!

Waging war on Jezebel is a hugely important issue in these last days because Jezebel's tactics are increasing and its goals are nowhere near completion. As a matter of fact, the methods of our archenemies will grow bigger and more vicious as we approach the end, because Satan knows his time is short (Revelation 12:12).

It is imperative, then, that every child of God be,

> Matthew 10:16 Behold, I send you forth as sheep in the midst of wolves: be ye therefore wise as serpents, and harmless as doves.

If we are to walk in victory, there is no room in the Church for the aggression of a Jezebel or the passivity of an

Ahab. We must live assertively, as Jesus did, and walk in the presence and power of the Holy Spirit as we discern and deal with this already defeated foe.

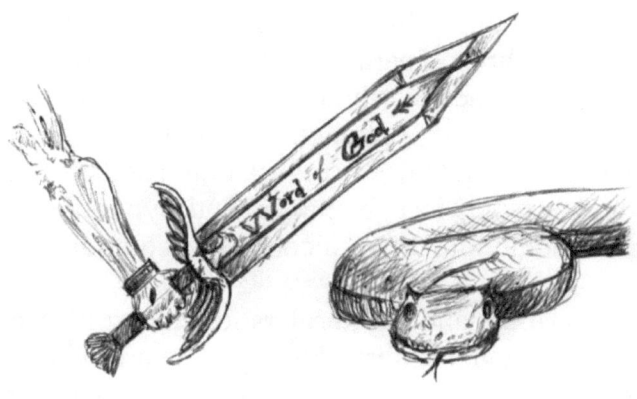

Prayer

I have revised a Breaking Witchcraft Prayer for you to use as a tool to overcome the spirit of Jezebel and all associated demonic activity.

In the name of Jesus Christ, my Lord and Savior, I bind all principalities, powers of the air, wickedness in high places, powers, thrones, dominions, world rulers, and strongmen, Jezebel or witchcraft exerting influence over _____(person or persons prayed for) and I forbid them to operate against the one praying this prayer.

I bind and break witchcraft, witchcraft control, mind binding spirits, spirits that block and/or bind the will, mind control, destruction, lust, fantasy lust, perversion, intimidation, rebellion, rejection, schizophrenia, paranoia, anger, hatred, wrath and rage, resentment bitterness, unforgiveness, unsearchableness, deception, doubt and unbelief, passivity, pride, jealousy, generational curses and false humility. I bind and break the spirits of Ahab and Jezebel, fear, hypnosis, and hypnotic trance, rock music, greed, addiction, drugs, alcohol, and compulsive behavior.

I bind kings, princes and world rulers for each spirit here named. I strip each spirit and his hierarchy of power, armor and rank, and separate each from the other. I speak confusion to the ranks of the enemy, and declare their assignments against _____ are hereby rendered null and void. I bind and break all evil affecting the senses of sight, smell, taste, touch, hearing; all evil against the seven points of the body used by witchcraft—base of the spine, spleen, navel, heart, throat, between the eyes and top of the head. I bind and break all evil on the systems of the body reproductive, skeletal, muscular, digestive, respiratory, circulatory, and nervous systems.

I bind and break any and all evil powers giving aid or pulling these systems in our bodies towards the evil by means of energy drawn from the sun, moon, planets, constellations, earth, air, wind, fire, water, light, darkness, matter, elements… or from lines, squares, circles, symbols, artifacts or potions used against us.

I bind and break any transference of spirits in family, friends or associates of _____. (Name the names of the people from whom you forbid transference of spirits.) With the Sword of the Spirit I sever all evil soul ties between these persons and _____. I declare that the blood of Jesus covers _____ mind, emotions, and will, preventing these soul ties form ever being re-established. Every spirit named in this prayer is bound off each person prayed for, as well as for the person uttering this prayer, *(Mathew 18:18 Verily I say unto you, whatsoever ye shall bind on earth shall be bound in heaven: and whatsoever ye shall loose on earth shall be loosed in heaven.)*

This prayer is in effect also for every person whom those praying and those prayed for have come in contact with. Spirits for the nether world, spirits between, over, and around those praying and those prayed for, and all familiar spirits are completely bound and for bidden to manifest in the name of Jesus. I bind and break the powers of all curses spoken, all ritual or sacrifices, all divination, spells, meditations, and all sorcery or magic.

I loose the Spirit of the Lord—the Spirit of Wisdom, Understanding, Counsel, Might, Knowledge, and the Fear of the Lord. *(Isaiah 11:2 And the Spirit of the Lord shall rest upon Him, the Spirit of Wisdom and Understanding, Spirit of Counsel and Might, the Spirit of Knowledge and the Fear of the Lord;)* upon the persons praying this prayer and the persons prayed for, along with the Spirit of Mercy, Grace, and Peace. I place shields of faith over the minds of those persons to protect against infiltration from the end time mind control.

Thank you Father that no weapon the enemy forms against us shall prosper, because we are covered by the blood of Jesus Christ, and You put all things under His feet. *(Isaiah 54:17 No weapon formed against thee shall prosper; and every tongue that shall rise against thee in judgment thou shall condemn. This is the heritage of the servants of the Lord. Ephesians 1:22 And hath put all things under His feet and gave Him to be the head over all things to the church)* Because Christ dwells in us, we declare that greater is He that is in us than he that is in the world *(1John 4:4 Ye are of God, little children, and have overcome them: because greater is He in you, than he that is in the world.)* I release generational blessings from our inheritance of Jesus Christ in Jesus name, Amen.

About the Author

Bill Vincent is an Apostle and Author with Revival Waves of Glory Ministries in Litchfield, IL. Bill and his wife Tabitha work closely in every day ministry duties. Bill and Tabitha lead a team providing Apostolic over sight in all aspects of ministry, including service, personal ministry and Godly character.

Bill is a believer in Jesus Christ in the fullness of power with signs and wonders. Bill has an accurate prophetic gift, a powerful revelatory preaching anointing with miracles signs and wonders following.

Bill Vincent is no stranger to understanding the power of God, having spent over twenty years as a Minister with a strong prophetic anointing, which taught him the importance of deliverance by the power of God. Bill has more than thirty prophetic books available all over the world. Prior to starting his ministry, Revival Waves of Glory he spent the last few years as a Pastor of a Church and a traveling prophetic ministry.

Bill Vincent helps the Body of Christ to get closer to God while overcoming the enemy. Bill offers a wide range of writings and teachings from deliverance, to the presence of God and Apostolic cutting edge Church structure. Drawing on the power of the Holy Spirit through years of experience in Revival, Spiritual Sensitivity and deliverance ministry, Bill now focuses mainly on pursuing the Presence of God and breaking the power of the devil off of people's lives.

His book Defeating the Demonic Realm was published in 2011 and has since helped many people to overcome the spirits and curses of satan. Since then Bill's books have flooded the market with his writings released just like he prophesies the Word of the Lord.

Bill Vincent is a unique man of God whom has discovered; powerful ways to pursue God's presence, releasing revelations of the demonic realm and prophetic anointing through everything he does. Bill is always moving forward at a rapid pace and there is sure to be much more released by him in upcoming years.

Warfare Books

You can find these powerful books everywhere books are sold.

Recommended Books

By Bill Vincent

Overcoming Obstacles

Glory: Pursuing God's Presence

Defeating the Demonic Realm

Increasing Your Prophetic Gift

Increase Your Anointing

Keys to Receiving Your Miracle

The Supernatural Realm

Waves of Revival

Increase of Revelation and Restoration

The Resurrection Power of God

Discerning Your Call of God

Apostolic Breakthrough

Glory: Increasing God's Presence

Love is Waiting – Don't Let Love Pass You By

The Healing Power of God

Glory: Expanding God's Presence

Receiving Personal Prophecy

Signs and Wonders

Signs and Wonders Revelations

Children Stories

The Rapture

The Secret Place of God's Power

Building a Prototype Church

Breakthrough of Spiritual Strongholds

Glory: Revival Presence of God

Overcoming the Power of Lust

Glory: Kingdom Presence of God

Transitioning to the Prototype Church

The Stronghold of Jezebel

Healing After Divorce

A Closer Relationship With God

Cover Up and Save Yourself

Desperate for God's Presence

The War for Spiritual Battles

Spiritual Leadership

Global Warning

Millions of Churches

Destroying the Jezebel Spirit

Awakening of Miracles

Deception and Consequences Revealed

Are You a Follower of Christ

Don't Let the Enemy Steal from You!

A Godly Shaking

The Unsearchable Riches of Christ

Heaven's Court System

Satan's Open Doors

Armed for Battle

The Wrestler

Spiritual Warfare: Complete Collection

Growing In the Prophetic

Faith

The Angry Fighter's Story

Understanding Heaven's Court System

Web Site:

www.revivalwavesofgloryministries.com

www.ingramcontent.com/pod-product-compliance
Lightning Source LLC
Chambersburg PA
CBHW030518080526
44586CB00011B/235